A STUDENT SURVIVAL GUIDE

FOR END-TIMES EVANGELISM

GREG STIER

MOODY PUBLISHERS
CHICAGO

Book Design: Julia Ryan [DesignByJulia]
Some images copyright PhotoDisc and "www.arttoday.com"

Library of Congress Cataloging-in-Publication Data
Stier, Greg.
        Last chance : a student survival guide for end-times evangelism /
    Greg Stier.
        p. cm.
    ISBN 0-8024-1792-2
    1. Church group work with teenagers. 2. Eschatology. I. Title.

    BV4447 .S694 2003
    248'.5'0835--dc21

                                                    2002152475

1 3 5 7 9 10 8 6 4 2
Printed in the United States of America

To Mom

thanks for always giving me a last chance

CONTENTS

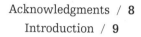

ACKNOWLEDGMENTS

To all the teenagers who have been to a Dare 2 Share conference throughout the years, I want to say thank you. Your adrenalin for Jesus and untapped potential give me the courage and determination to keep on keeping on in the wild and unpredictable world of student ministry.

To all the youth leaders who have helped shape and launch "the revolution," thanks. Most of you are overworked and underpaid, but one of your rewards is waiting in heaven. The other reward is the lives that God is using you to transform on earth. As Paul wrote in 1 Thessalonians 2:19–20, "For what is our hope, our joy, or the crown in which we will glory in the presence of our Lord Jesus when he comes? Is it not you? Indeed, you are our glory and joy."

Thanks as well to all the prayer warriors and donors who have made this ministry to students possible and powerful. Your partnership in the gospel is reaping a harvest of lives changed and souls saved. Only heaven knows the number of young lives your investment has reached.

INTRODUCTION

his may be your last chance. By the time you finish reading this introduction, Jesus could ride a cloud into the stratosphere of the blue sky above and give the nod for His angel to blow the trumpet. When that heavenly horn blasts its rallying signal, it will be too late. You will either be taken or left behind. Your friends will either be with you in the presence of God or left on this earth to endure the torments of God's wrath being poured out in full measure on the enemies of God. Does that scare you? It should. It scares me. 🎇

Fiction or fact? It may seem unreal. It may sound like the kind of stuff we can watch on the Sci-Fi channel, but it is not. It is gospel truth. It is all over the Bible. The Word of God is packed with prophecy . . . some fulfilled thousands of years ago and some yet to be fulfilled. One of the recurring themes of many of the prophecies in the Bible is that Jesus is coming soon to this planet. So the real question is not, Is it real? but, Are you ready? 🎇

ABOUT THIS BOOK

 ast Chance is a survival guide designed to make you Rapture-ready. It will give you some basic instruction on what the end times are really all about. It will prepare you to live and give the gospel to those around you with a sense of urgency. It will motivate and equip you to share your faith with your friends before it's too late.

We will not try to guess the exact day or time that Jesus may be coming back. Only God knows that. Those who say they know don't. Even Jesus said, "It is not for you to know the times or dates the Father has set by his own authority. But you will receive power when the Holy Spirit comes on you; and you will be my witnesses in Jerusalem, and in all Judea and Samaria, and to the ends of the earth" (Acts 1:7–8).

In other words, Jesus is saying that we shouldn't worry about the exact day Jesus is coming back but rather that we should be focusing on reaching every person on this planet with the gospel of Jesus Christ before He comes back! Our mission is to start with those around us and not stop witnessing until the "ends of the earth" are shaken with the gospel of Jesus Christ. As you are reading this book I want you to remember this key point. It's not about just learning a bunch of facts about prophecy. It's about the reality of the Rapture and the end times motivating us to live and witness with urgency.

When you finish reading this book you will know a lot more about prophecy. You will understand some of the basic biblical truths about the end times. But more than anything else you will know how to share your faith anytime, anywhere, with anyone. You will have no excuses to keep your mouth shut about Jesus anymore.

So how about it, teenager? Are you ready to hear the trumpet blast? Are you living a life so impassioned for God that you wouldn't blush if you were suddenly transported into His presence? Are you reaching your friends with the gospel before it's too late? Are you ready to launch?

Coming soon to a planet near you . . . Jesus.

HOW TO USE THIS BOOK

 don't know about you, but I love the TV reality show *Survivor.* For the three of you who haven't seen it yet, let me give a brief rundown of the show and its purpose. Sixteen pre-chosen contestants are brought to a remote location (desert, jungle, island, wilderness, etc.) where they compete against each other individually and as teams. The winners of the tribal challenges receive some kind of special prize or privilege. But the real goal is to win immunity from the Tribal Council. During this dramatic nighttime meeting one person is voted off on each show.

I watch this show riveted (along with millions of others) as alliances form and break, as some advance on and others are voted off. It culminates in one survivor who wins one million dollars at the end of the series.

What I like about the show is the strange balance of individual and team competition that results in all sorts of wacky dynamics. These individual and team competitions are sort of like life. There are things that we do together and things we do alone.

With that in mind I have developed an action plan at the end of each chapter that combines individual and team effort. You see, this book was made for you to go through individually and as a team. Whether that team is a campus ministry or a youth group or just a couple of friends, this book was designed to be tribal. You read it on your own, and that's where the personal challenge is faced to share your faith. But you also read it as a community of believers who are going to work together for the winning of the ultimate prize . . . the glory of God. ❇

So there are three different sections at the end of each chapter. One is meant for you and you alone. The other two are meant for the tribe. But one thing each of these sections has in common is this . . . they are meant to be acted on. ❇

Let's take a look at each action section at the end of each chapter:

STUDENT SURVIVAL TIPS

This section is designed to give you some personal action steps that you can apply right away in your own life to make you effective at doing what you just learned in the chapter that you just read. It is personal. It is practical. It is action-driven. ❇

WORST-CASE SCENARIOS

This part of the action section gives you at least one worst-case scenario and sometimes gives hints for how to overcome it. It is designed to go through as a group, and it contains questions that will help you work your way through this worst-case scenario to a powerful and practical solution. ❇

The Tribal Challenge

This gives your whole team one thing to do as a tribe with the material that you just learned. It is not easy. But those tribes that take the challenge and win will reap the rewards. ✠

Again, this book is meant to be tribal as well as individual. Why? Because that is the same way God deals with us. He calls us to individual as well as communal obedience. He asks us to serve Him personally and in the context of the "tribe" called the church. You need to think of your youth group and/or campus ministry and/or circle of Christian friends as a tribe competing for the ultimate prize . . . not a million dollars but the billions of souls on this planet who still don't know Jesus Christ as their Savior. ✠

Because the real tribe is not just the fellow students you go to youth group with or the Christian friends you have in school. The leaders of the tribe are the Father, Son, and Holy Spirit as they work together with you to make you an effective witness to the gospel in the end times. And one day soon we will stand before the ultimate tribal council . . . the judgment seat of Christ. On that day all of our actions will be evaluated to determine the degree of reward that we will have as we enter into heaven with God forever and ever. And the ultimate reward will be hearing the words "Well done, my good and faithful servant." That's the only thing that matters. That we served Christ with all of our heart, soul, mind, and might while on the earth and that we hear the words "well done." That's what the action section is all about . . . to help you do well in life, the ultimate survivor challenge.

The tribe has spoken.

1

"I'LL BE BACK"

✵ IN *TERMINATOR* 1 AND 2 A MUSCLE-BOUND
ARNOLD SCHWARZENEGGER, PLAYING THE ROLE
OF A POWERFUL CYBORG FROM THE FUTURE, POP-
ULARIZED THE SLOGAN "I'LL BE BACK." I'M SURE
THAT T 3 WILL BE COMING SOON TO A THEATER

NEAR YOU. BUT TWO THOUSAND YEARS BEFORE ARNOLD EVER FLEXED ONTO MOVIE SCREENS ACROSS THE GLOBE, THE MOST POWERFUL BEING IN THE UNIVERSE SAID THE SAME THING IN A DIFFERENT WAY. IN JOHN 14:3 JESUS CHRIST TOLD HIS DISCIPLES, "IF I GO AND PREPARE A PLACE FOR YOU, **I WILL COME BACK** AND TAKE YOU TO BE WITH ME THAT YOU ALSO MAY BE WHERE I AM" *(bold emphasis added).* ✠

It's not a matter of *if* Jesus is returning but *when* He is returning. Now, I don't believe that we as Christians should be trying to guess when Jesus is coming back to take us to heaven, but I think we should be ready all the time. Somebody once said that we should live as though "Christ died yesterday, rose again this morning, and is coming back again tonight." He will be back. And all of the signs are pointing to the fact that it could be very, very soon. ✠

THE FUTURE IN PROPHECY

Did you know that there is not one more prophecy that needs to be fulfilled before Jesus comes back, as far as I know? In other words, the stage is set. Stop and think about it for a moment. Jesus said that right before the end of days there would be "wars and rumors of wars." Just sit down and watch the news sometime. From the war against terrorism here and abroad to the Middle East conflicts to the countless other battles, skirmishes, and factions, globally the stage is set for the coming of Jesus and the beginning of the end. ✠

Where were you during 9-11? ✠

I remember where I was. I was sitting in a Starbucks doing some writing when my wife called with the disturbing news that something bad was taking place in New York City. I rushed home and watched in horror along with the rest of America as the second plane hit and then as each tower collapsed into a pile of rubble. I don't think any of us will ever be the same after that shocking morning. The terrorist attacks we heard about on CNN that seemed a million miles away had now come to U.S. soil. It had hit home . . . literally. But this is just the beginning.

The Bible paints a very graphic and horrible picture of global conflicts and natural catastrophes that will slaughter billions of people during the time of Tribulation described in the book of Revelation. The events of 9-11 are a sneak preview of the pain and struggle and trouble to come. Fasten your seatbelts. It just gets worse from here for those who don't know Christ.

ONE-WORLD GOVERNMENT

Not only that, but for the first time in the history of humanity we have the technology to truly have a one-world government. The book of Revelation talks about a united planet under the leadership of the Antichrist that will take a final, futile stand against the people of God (Revelation 16:14–16). Technology has made the world "smaller." Before airplanes you would have had to take the slow boat to China. Now you can do a live Webcast globally with the click of a mouse.

American-made movies and music have become the universal language. From India to Japan to Russia, our music and movies have shaped culture. The Americanization of the world has begun and expanded through America's impact on culture. Almost everywhere you go on this planet people have the common ground of music and movies. �skⱻ

The Internet has done the same thing. It has made the world smaller through a computer screen. The information superhighway has created a way for a teenager in America to chat with a teenager in Poland, Saudi Arabia, or China. Think about www . . . the *world wide* web. It is a global communications system that has united the planet in ways that one hundred years ago were unthinkable. ✻

This global unity is absolutely necessary for the devil's plan to bring together the world to take a stand against God in the Battle of Armageddon at the end of the Tribulation. This showdown won't last long. As a matter of fact, here is what the Bible says about it: "And then the lawless one will be revealed, whom the Lord Jesus will overthrow with the breath of his mouth and destroy by the splendor of his coming" (2 Thessalonians 2:8). In other words, all Jesus has to do is show up and the battle is over. But for the battle to even begin, the road to global unity must be paved years before. The information superhighway is part of the asphalt. So are music and movies. So is the move toward a global currency. So are a whole bunch of other things. ✻

THE MARK OF THE BEAST

The mark of the Beast now seems reasonable and feasible. During the time of Tribulation on the earth the Antichrist will force everyone to receive a mark. Without the mark people won't be able to buy or sell anything (Revelation 13:16–17). They will be shunned from society and eventually killed (Revelation 20:4). 🎴

The technology is close to being able to be enacted to mark everybody in the world. Maybe this mark will be kind of a social security card combined with an ATM card combined with a GPS Tracking System microchip. With this mark on your right hand or forehead you could scan your hand or head at Blockbuster's to rent your latest movie. It would immediately deduct the amount you owed from your bank account. Not only that, but the powers that be would learn your spending habits because cash would be a thing of the past. 🎴

Ever see the movie *Enemy of the State* with Will Smith? With strategically placed pieces of technology planted on his body it was difficult for him to get away from the "eye in the sky." But what if those pieces of technology were planted *in* his body (right hand or forehead)? It would be impossible to get away from "them." 🎴

A POSSIBLE SCENARIO

Imagine with me what the end times could be like. There is a huge "vanishing" of billions of people all over the world in one instant. Some say it is an unexplained scientific phenomenon. Others say that aliens have abducted these people for unknown reasons—all these years of UFO sightings finally make sense; they were planning a cosmic abduction of biblical proportions. Still others say that it was the "Rapture" referred to in the Bible. Most people don't know. But one thing they know for sure: Havoc has struck.

Part of the global problem is that the economy is thrown into a recession like never seen before in history. Not only that, but thousands or even millions have died in the sudden crashes of unmanned aircrafts, cars, and trucks. In addition this vanishing has also seemed to spark some kind of catastrophe epidemic: comets crashing to the earth, tornadoes, earthquakes, famine, and volcanoes. Worldwide panic has led to looting and a crime wave that has swept the entire globe.

Everything looks like it is leading to utter destruction when all of a sudden one powerful leader takes control. He has unique powers and a winsome personality. He seems to have the answers. "Let's unite the world and fight these troubles together" is his solution. Working with the most powerful leaders of the most powerful nations, he enacts an emergency action strategy that declares kind of a global martial law. Part of that plan is to make sure everyone is "marked" with a code that goes into a universal computer system. With this mark people can buy, sell, and live freely. Without it they will be hunted down and killed. Why? Because the only ones, in his explanation, who wouldn't want it are the looters, the killers, and the criminals who have become such a problem.

This means that those who have become Christians since the Rapture would be seen as criminals immediately. They would become "enemies of the state" and tracked down and terminated. ▓

To be honest, I don't know for sure that this is going to be the exact scenario that will be played out, but the point is that it finally makes sense why the mark would be used, and it seems feasible on a technological level. The end-times catastrophes mentioned in the book of Revelation could be right around the corner! ▓

All that to say this . . . stuff is in place for Jesus to come back. ▓

THE FULFILLMENT OF
ALL PROPHECY

What's all this talk about prophecy, anyway? ▓

Before we launch into our discussion of future events we should understand a few things about prophecy itself. First of all, prophecy is a declaration of truth. In the Old Testament, prophets often would say "Thus saith the Lord" and then prove it with a prediction about the future. Some of these predictions were about the immediate future. Others were about the distant future. For instance, did you know that the book of Daniel makes very specific predictions about both the immediate and distant future? ▓

PROPHECIES FULFILLED IN
THE PAST

The book of Daniel was written by the prophet Daniel in the sixth century before Christ. He predicted the establishment of the Babylonian, the Medo-Persian, the Grecian, and the Roman kingdoms, in that order (Daniel 2). He also predicted the coming of Alexander the Great and the four scheming generals who would take over after his death (Daniel 8), and he gave very specific prophecies concerning their battles with each other (Daniel 11). Daniel even predicted the exact time of Jesus' death hundreds of years before He was born (Daniel 9:25–26). ✖

Those "experts" who don't believe that the Bible is from God do everything they can to try to explain the book of Daniel away because the prophecies he made were fulfilled literally with exacting detail. They can't handle the truth, so they develop elaborate explanations about this book being forged by somebody else later on. But this is just the beginning of their problems. ✖

The whole Old Testament is filled with prophecies, many of which have been literally fulfilled already. These are prophecies like where Christ would be born (Micah 5:2) and how He would die (Psalm 22). As a matter of fact, the chances of just forty-eight of the hundreds of Old Testament prophecies about Christ to be literally fulfilled in one person is 1 in 10^{157} power. That's one of ten with one hundred and fifty-six zeroes behind it. That is the same statistical probability of one person randomly picking one pre-marked atom hidden in one trillion, trillion, trillion, trillion, billion universes.[1] In other words, the odds are against those who think that biblical prophecy is a joke. �֎

And believe me, the list goes on and on and on with prophecies that have been fulfilled literally in the Bible. These prophecies are not ones like Nostradamus made. He wrote his prophecies in a hidden code that was poetic, dark, mysterious, and confusing. The few prophecies that he kind of came close on pale in comparison to biblical prophecy. When God used a prophet to make a prediction, He demanded 100 percent accuracy. Listen to these words from God: "You may say to yourselves, 'How can we know when a message has not been spoken by the LORD?' If what a prophet proclaims in the name of the LORD does not take place or come true, that is a message the LORD has not spoken. That prophet has spoken presumptuously. Do not be afraid of him" (Deuteronomy 18:21–22). In other words, God demanded 100 percent accuracy of His prophets. �֎

People listen to the prophecies of Nostradamus and look at how many he got right. Instead they should be asking if he got any wrong. He got thousands wrong. If he had been an Old Testament prophet, the Israelites would have stoned him. ✖

PROPHECIES THAT HAVE NOT BEEN FULFILLED YET

What's the point of all this? That we can believe the prophecies God made for the future times in the book of

Revelation (and other books in the Old and New Testament) based on His track record of success in the past when it comes to prophecy that has already been fulfilled.

God never asks us to have "blind faith." He gives us reasons to believe. The hundreds of prophecies that have been literally fulfilled give us strong reason to believe that the future end-times prophecy will be fulfilled just as He predicted through His prophets.

So what are some of those future prophecies?

Let me boil them down to a handful for you to have a framework for future prophecy:

1 JESUS IS COMING BACK SOON!

The Bible makes it clear that Jesus is going to come back to the earth again. Acts 1:9–11 paints a vivid picture of how He will come back.

*fter he [Jesus] said this, he was taken up before their very eyes, and a cloud hid him from their sight. They were looking intently up into the sky as he was going, when suddenly two men dressed in white stood beside them. "Men of Galilee," they said, "why do you stand here looking into the sky? This same Jesus, who has been taken from you into heaven, will come back **in the same way** you have seen him go into heaven." (bold emphasis added)*

Jesus ascended into heaven physically and disappeared into a cloud after His resurrection. When He returns He will descend from a cloud onto the earth. That day will be a great and awesome day of judgment on the earth. As a matter of fact, throughout Scripture it is called the Day of the Lord. It is when those who reject Jesus Christ as their Savior will meet their doom. It will be a scary, scary time for those who don't know the Lord. Listen to how the Bible describes it.

ee, the day of the LORD is coming—a cruel day, with wrath and fierce anger—to make the land desolate and destroy the sinners within it. The stars of heaven and their constellations will not show their light. The rising sun will be darkened and the moon will not give its light. I will punish the world for its evil, the wicked for their sins. I will put an end to the arrogance of the haughty and will humble the pride of the ruthless. I will make man scarcer than pure gold, more rare than the gold of Ophir. Therefore I will make the heavens tremble; and the earth will shake from its place at the wrath of the LORD Almighty, in the day of his burning anger. (Isaiah 13:9–13)

2 THERE IS A COMING TIME OF TRIBULATION THAT WILL COME BEFORE JESUS' RETURN TO THE EARTH.

This seven-year time of trouble, calamity, disaster, and catastrophe will be a horrible time on the earth. Just read the book of Revelation (especially chapters 4–19) to get a taste of the judgment that will be poured out on the earth during this terrible time. It is during this seven-year period that the Antichrist will unite the world under his control to fight against the people of God in Jerusalem. At the very end of this Tribulation time Jesus will return to earth (the Day of the Lord), defeat the Antichrist, and set up His kingdom on the earth. We will rule and reign with Him forever and ever. It will be awesome! Check this out . . .

nd then the lawless one [the Antichrist] will be revealed, whom the Lord Jesus will overthrow with the breath of his mouth and destroy by the splendor of his coming. The coming of the lawless one will be in accordance with the work of Satan displayed in all kinds of counterfeit miracles, signs and wonders. (2 Thessalonians 2:8–9)

The Antichrist will unite the world under his power by impressing everyone with all of his counterfeit miracles. He will make everyone receive his mark on their right hands or foreheads (Revelation 13:16–18). Only the Christians will refuse his mark, and they will be hunted down like animals as a result. But in the end the Antichrist and his followers (those who receive his mark) will be destroyed and thrown into the lake of fire. ✠

f anyone worships the beast and his image and receives his mark on the forehead or on the hand, he, too, will drink of the wine of God's fury, which has been poured full strength into the cup of his wrath. He will be tormented with burning sulfur in the presence of the holy angels and of the Lamb. And the smoke of their torment rises for ever and ever. There is no rest day or night for those who worship the beast and his image, or for anyone who receives the mark of his name. (Revelation 14:9–11)

Pretty serious stuff. But you have nothing to worry about, if you have trusted in Jesus Christ as your Savior—the mark of God is on your soul so the mark of the Beast could never be on your hand or head. That brings us to the third point. 🞧

3   JESUS WILL "RAPTURE" HIS CHURCH FROM THE COMING JUDGMENT.

You may be kind of freaking out after reading all of this fire and brimstone stuff. But if you are a believer, don't worry . . . Jesus will rescue you. Christians have nicknamed this rescuing "the Rapture." It is described in 1 Thessalonians 4:16–18, *or the Lord himself will come down from heaven, with a loud command, with the voice of the archangel and with the trumpet call of God, and the dead in Christ will rise first. After that, we who are still alive and are left will be caught up together with them in the clouds to meet the Lord in the air. And so we will be with the Lord forever. Therefore encourage each other with these words.*

Here is the deal. Jesus will come back in the clouds, cue His main angel to give a call on his trumpet, and all the bodies of the believers who have died will come blasting through their coffins, through the six feet of ground above them, and be transformed into their glorified bodies (1 Corinthians 15:51–52). Just last week I buried my grandmother. As I officiated the graveside service and looked down into the pit where her flower-covered coffin lay, I thought of that day . . . that day that her body would burst through the metal coffin that encased her body . . . that day when her newly trans-formed and glorified body will burst through the ground and into the sky to meet the Lord in the air. I wonder what it will be like for someone planting flowers at the cemetery that day!

But the resurrection of the dead is not the end of the Rapture story. Immediately following their transforma-tion and flight into the heavens, those who are still alive will be "raptured" from the earth and meet all the Christians from the past and the present and Jesus Himself in the clouds. That will be the biggest reunion in the history of mankind. I can't wait for that day! ❈

When will the Rapture take place? Nobody knows. That's the point. Jesus could return at *any* time, so we need to be ready *all* the time. We need to live holy lives and share the gospel message with urgency because Jesus is coming soon! ❈

Will He come back before, during, or after the Tribulation time? This has been a subject of great debate among Christians for a long time. Some believe that Jesus will come back before the seven-year Tribulation. (As you can tell, that's the position I take.) Others believe that He will come back in the middle of the Tribulation, and still others believe He will come at the end. There are some who believe that we will not be raptured and that the earth will not go through the great Tribulation. They believe that He will return to the earth and judge the living and the dead and that's it. ❈

I encourage you to study your Bible, talk to your youth pastor, ask God to reveal His truth to you through His Holy Spirit, and come to your own conclusions. What matters most is that you believe that Jesus is coming back soon and that you need to be ready. There are many, many viewpoints of end-times prophecy. But there is ultimately only one major point of all future prophecy. ❈

THE POINT OF ALL PROPHECY

We can talk about the finer points of future prophecy all day and all night and still not agree. We can argue about when the Rapture will take place. We can dialogue about the seven-year time of trouble and tribulation on the earth. We can speculate about whether the Rapture will take place before, during, or toward the end of the Tribulation. We can debate about the thousand-year reign of Christ on the earth called the "Millennium." We can talk about all of this stuff and still miss *the* point of all prophecy . . . be ready! ✠

All future prophecy motivates us to be ready because Jesus is coming back soon. He could come back at any time. Sometimes the smart people of Christianity who go to seminary and know a lot of stuff miss this main point of prophecy. They are so busy debating the finer points that they miss the main point! We as believers are called to live with a sense of holy anticipation, knowing that Jesus could interrupt history at any second. This sense of eagerness should produce in us a holy fear of sin and a passionate pursuit of those who don't know Jesus. It should help us to put things in perspective. What matters most is not the kind of car we drive or clothes we wear, but how much we are serving the Lord Jesus Christ. ✠

In the last chapter of the last book of the Bible Jesus says, "Behold, I am coming soon! Blessed is he who keeps the words of the prophecy in this book" (Revelation 22:7). Jesus is saying that the whole point of the book of Revelation is to remind us that He is coming soon, so we need to be obedient to His Word and live our Christianity like we mean it! ✠

What does that kind of Christianity look like? It is a Christianity that looks to the clouds and looks to the crowds. If you are outside or by a window right now, look out to the sky and try to find a cloud. Now think to yourself this amazing thought: *Jesus could be on that cloud right now with an army of His servants waiting to cue His archangel to blow the trumpet and call us home.* When we look up to the clouds we also look into our lives. We see the hidden, secret sins that we would be totally embarrassed by if we were suddenly transported into the presence of Jesus. ❖

Now look to the people around you right now. If you are by a street, look at the cars driving by. If you are in a neighborhood, look at the houses around you that are filled with people. If you are at school, look up and see the other teenagers in the hallway, cafeteria, or classroom. Do they know Jesus? If not, once that trumpet blows it will be too late for you to tell them. We need to tell our friends about Jesus before it's too late. Look to the clouds and look to the crowds. The rest of this book will help you do just that. ❖

NOTE
1. Lee Strobel, *Inside the Mind of Unchurched Harry & Mary* (Grand Rapids: Zondervan, 1993), p.31

Student Survival Tips

1. Make sure that you know Jesus Christ as your Savior so that you aren't left behind to suffer the judgment of God! (If you need to, jump ahead to pages 70-73 and find out how you can know for sure that you will be rescued out of the coming trouble!)

2. Ask yourself this question: "Which of my friends do I think would be left behind if the Rapture happened today?" Write their names down.

3. Are you ready for Jesus to return? If not, why not?

Worst-Case Scenario

WHAT TO DO IN CASE YOU ARE LEFT BEHIND

You wake up one day to find out that tens of millions of people have disappeared from the face of the earth. There is global calamity and mass hysteria everywhere. Some say "alien abduction" or "scientific phenomenon," but you know better. It is the Rapture and you have been left behind.

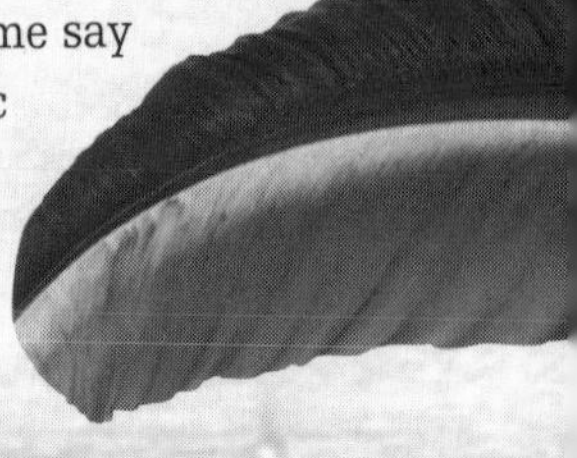

What are the action steps you would go through right away?

1.

2.

3.

4.

How would you choose to "survive" during this time of global catastrophe? (Check out these passages for help: Matthew 24:15–21 and Revelation 13:5–10.) ▦

What can we do to make sure that we and our family and friends don't go through this horrible time? ▦

THE TRIBAL CHALLENGE

Take one hour and read the whole book of Revelation together out loud using an easy-to-understand translation. (Make sure all of you read from the same version to avoid confusion.) As each person is reading a different section, the others write down their thoughts on a piece of paper. Have everybody share their thoughts with each other afterward. ▦

THE REAL MIB

2

⊞ WHAT IF THE UNIVERSE WERE FULL OF BLOOD-THIRSTY ALIENS WHO WANTED NOTHING MORE THAN TO RIP THIS WORLD APART? WHAT IF YOU WERE CALLED TO BE A PART OF AN UNDER-GROUND SOCIETY OF AGENTS WHOSE SOLE MISSION

WAS TO WIPE OUT THE GLOBAL THREAT THROUGH COVERT OPERATIONS AND DIRECT ATTACK? WHAT IF YOU WERE LOADED WITH SPECIAL WEAPONS THAT WOULD ENABLE YOU TO FIGHT AND WIN AGAINST THESE ENE- MIES NO MATTER HOW BIG AND BAD THEY APPEARED? ✠

Did you know that someday in the near future God will unleash His own version of Men in Black across the planet? Their mission is simple . . . to protect the earth from the scum of the universe. How do they do that? During the Tribulation time on the earth they preach the gospel of Jesus Christ to every person on the planet. Their goal is to save the soul. That is all that they are about. The word "Father" is stamped on their foreheads, the message of the gospel tattooed on their souls, and the blazing passion to witness burning in their souls. These spiritual MIB invade the world with the gospel of Jesus Christ. While the Antichrist is raising up his army of evil, they will be raising up an army of believers. ✠

Maybe this, too, sounds like the stuff of science fiction. So let me give you some biblical proof. Listen to these verses.

hen I looked, and there before me was the Lamb, standing on Mount Zion, and with him 144,000 who had his name and his Father's name written on their foreheads . . . the 144,000 who had been redeemed from the earth. These are those who did not defile themselves with women, for they kept them- selves pure. (Revelation 14:1, 3–4)

In Revelation 7 we find out that these 144,000 male virgins are from the tribes of Israel. We also find out that right after they appear on the scene, a whole bunch of people appear in heaven.

After this [the appearance of the 144,000 "MIB" on earth] I looked and there before me was a great multitude that no one could count, from every nation, tribe, people and language, standing before the throne and in front of the Lamb. They were wearing white robes and were holding palm branches in their hands. (Revelation 7:9)

Who was this great multitude? "These are they who have come out of the great tribulation" (Revelation 7:14). In other words, these are those who had become believers during the Tribulation and had been transported into the presence of God. How did they become believers? Someone preached the gospel to them. Who preached the gospel? I am convinced that it was the 144,000 MIB! It makes sense that when the 144,000 MIB are unleashed on earth that suddenly countless people appear in heaven—killed by the Antichrist for being Christians and refusing to take the mark of the beast. (The Antichrist can't touch or harm the 144,000 MIB, by the way.)

I want you to imagine how passionate these MIB will be to preach the gospel to lead such a large crowd to Christ! If there were only four billion people on the earth after the Rapture takes place, it would take each MIB preaching the gospel to more than 27,000 people apiece for every person in the world to hear the gospel once. And all of this witnessing is done over a pretty short period of time.

What's my point? Buckle your seatbelt. You are in for a surprise. That is then. This is now! Today we don't have 144,000 male Jewish virgins traveling the planet preaching the gospel to everything that moves. We have you and me. We are the real MIBs today! We are the ones who are called to preach the gospel to the world. We are the ones who are called to take on the scum of the universe with the truth of God's Word! ✖

The world is filled with bloodthirsty aliens called demons who want to shred this world and dominate it for their own evil purposes. You are part of an underground network of Christians who are called to wipe this threat out through covert prayer and direct-attack evangelism. God has equipped you with the weapons of intercession, worship, His Word, and the gospel to wage war against the scum of the universe . . . Satan himself. You are the real MIB. You are the real warrior of the cosmos, serving your King, and through His strength protecting the world from the Prince of Darkness. ✖

These MIB of the book of Revelation are focused on a mission of proclamation and purity. They proclaim the gospel to an unsaved world and live a life of purity in front of them. In the same way, if we are going to be like them, we must learn to invade and persuade (proclaim) and deal and heal (purity). ✖

INVADE AND PERSUADE

Just like the MIB of the book of Revelation, we have a mission that seems impossible . . . to reach every person on the planet with the gospel of Jesus Christ and to rescue them from the clutches of the Evil One. Jesus said,

All authority in heaven and on earth has been given to me. Therefore go and make disciples of all nations, baptizing them in the name of the Father and of the Son and of the Holy Spirit, and teaching them to obey everything I have commanded you. And surely I am with you always, to the very end of the age. (Matthew 28:18–20)

This mission is clear, dangerous, and extreme. It is going to take teenagers who are just as intense to accomplish this quest. It is going to take teenagers just like you who are tired of just going to church and want to start doing Christianity. You know the difference, right? Try reading the book of Acts and then going to church. Talk about a letdown!

In the book of Acts there was an urgency and intensity. Those early believers thought that Jesus was going to come back at any time, and they witnessed with a holy intensity that would blow the typical church away. Something has gone drastically wrong!

For ten and a half years I was a preaching pastor to adults at a church I helped plant. That church is an awesome church with all sorts of people coming to Christ. But after Columbine I resigned with the sudden realization that if there was going to be real revival in the church then teens were going to have to be a huge part of it. Many adults are too stuck in their ways, concerned about their stuff, and unwilling to take risks. I realized that if there was truly going to be a spiritual movement of biblical proportions it was going to take both wise and godly adults modeling an authentic Christianity and teenagers who were willing to push the envelope by taking risks and being extreme in reaching their communities for Christ! The church needed its people who were risk taking, extreme, and bordering on the obnoxious . . . teenagers! 🏁

Every major awakening in the history of the United States has had teenagers on the leading edge of that revival. Why? They are idealistic and unrealistic and ready for the challenge. They don't want to start a subcommittee investigating the potential and viable strategies of reaching a certain demographic—they want to do something! That's why my full-time job is unleashing teenagers, just like you, to do something with the gospel . . . to invade and persuade. 🏁

God has chosen you for this very special purpose. "But you are a chosen people, a royal priesthood, a holy nation, a people belonging to God, that you may declare the praises of him who called you out of darkness into his wonderful light" (1 Peter 2:9). 🏁

Maybe you don't feel like you are special. In your thinking you don't compare to the popular, beautiful, or "cool" at your school. But in God's estimation (which is really the only one that matters) you are so unique that you were handcrafted by God Himself in your mother's womb (Psalm 139:13–14). He handpicked you for a special purpose: "that you may declare the praises of him who called you out of darkness." In other words, God made you special at birth and made you for a special purpose when you were "born again" spiritually. What is that special purpose? To invade your world and persuade everyone you come in contact with to become a Christian! 🏁

Did you know that suicide has increased among high school students by more than 300 percent in the last thirty years? Chances are you know of somebody in your school who has slammed the pills, pulled the trigger, or knotted the rope. The hopelessness that is rampant in the lives of many of these teenagers flows from a feeling of personal worthlessness. You never have to feel that way. You have been crafted by the Creator and chosen by the Lord Jesus Christ for a very special purpose. You have a reason to live. ✠

And come on! Most of us have had thoughts about suicide at one time or another! I have. I will never forget the first time I ever had those evil thoughts of suicide bouncing around in my brain. And, of course, it was over a girl in high school that I was in "love" with who wouldn't return the favor. I thought about just ending it all. The main reason I didn't was the realization that God had chosen me for a purpose. The more I thought about His unending love for me, the less that girl's love (or lack thereof) seemed important. Those fleeting thoughts of suicide were destroyed by the love of God and the security and significance I found in Him. ✠

Maybe you are going through a time of emotional trauma in your life. Maybe it's a relational situation with a boyfriend or girlfriend or mom or dad. Or maybe you have been abused in some way and you feel that you will never recover. Perhaps it's just kind of a deep and steady pain in your heart that has been there for a long time and you have no answer as to why it is there. Maybe you look in the mirror and you don't like what you see. ✠

Whatever pain you may have in your heart, take some time and focus on God's unchanging love for you. He made you just the way you are and loves you just the way you are (although of course His goal is for you to be more and more like Christ all the time). He chose you for a purpose . . . to share His good news with those who have no hope. His goal is to use your life in unimaginable ways to advance His kingdom and His cause. Forget the pills, the gun, or the rope, and instead lose your life in the Book. As Jesus said, when you lose your life in Him you find what real life is all about (Mark 8:35). ✠

DEAL AND HEAL

If you are going to effectively invade and persuade, then you need to learn how to walk in a way that pleases God with your mind and body. In other words, you need to learn how to deal and heal when it comes to sexual purity . . . because the world is watching. ✠

 ear friends, I urge you, as aliens and strangers in the world, to abstain from sinful desires, which war against your soul. Live such good lives among the pagans that, though they accuse you of doing wrong, they may see your good deeds and glorify God on the day he visits us. (1 Peter 2:11–12)

The MIB of the future will be virgins. They are men who are sexually pure and driven by a passion for holiness. They refuse to let themselves get into compromising situations with members of the opposite sex (or same sex for that matter). They have a passion for purity and are marked by holiness. They are famous for their purity. This purity becomes their "suit" that they wear everywhere they go. It is recognized by everyone they come into contact with across the planet. It is their distinguishing mark. It is what sets them apart from the rest of the world. That is then. This is now.

You are called to be a real member of the MIB, not only in the sense that you have been chosen to be a part of a very specific team with a very specific purpose (the proclamation of the gospel of Jesus Christ, and thereby "protecting the earth from the scum of the universe"), but you have a very specific "suit" to wear. It is the suit of sexual purity.

Just as MIB in the movie can be easily identified by their black suits and cool glasses, the real MIB of the future (the 144,000) and today (you) can be easily picked out of a crowd by their sexual purity.

Therein lies the problem. Today's Christian teenager is not much different when it comes to sexual purity from today's non-Christian teenager. That's right—there is no significant lifestyle difference between those who claim to be Christians and those who don't when it comes to sexual purity!

What was meant to be one of the main distinguishing characteristics of the Rapture-ready Christian (sexual purity) has been erased in the tidal wave of compromise that has doused the flames of passion for God and crushed the testimony of the body of Christ to a watching world.

A WORD TO THE BROTHERS

So what about you guys? Are you sexually pure? Do you have secret, hidden habits of masturbation and pornography? Are you steeped in a relationship with a member of the opposite or same sex that is crossing the line of sexual purity? If so, then know this: You have damaged not only your relationship with God and the fabric of your own soul, but you have stripped away your power to persuade a watching world. If you are no different in your lifestyle and habits than your unchurched friends are, then why would they want what you have? Maybe you need a fresh start. Confess your sin to God, receive His forgiveness, and then have a godly, older man in your church keep you accountable. Jesus died for all of our sins . . . our sexual sins included. So receive your fresh start from Him!

A WORD TO THE SISTERS

And ladies, what about you? Are you sexually pure? Do you secretly fantasize about romantic relationships that lead to sexual thoughts that are out-of-bounds? Are you longing for relational fulfillment and finding it in sexual activity? Are your core heart needs being fulfilled by a guy with an agenda for your body or the God "guy," Jesus Christ, who has an agenda for your soul?

HOW TO DEAL AND HEAL

Guys and girls must learn to *deal and heal.* Christian teens must understand that if they are going to be witnesses of the life-changing power of Jesus Christ, then they themselves must have their lives changed. In the sexual arena, this comes as a result of learning to deal with current sexual temptation and to heal from any past sexual compromise.

Dealing with sexual temptation is no easy task. (And don't let anyone tell you that it is!) Sexual temptation is a driving, *almost* unstoppable force that starts in the teenage years and never, ever stops! Many teens when they first enter into this hormonal battle of urges and surges don't know how to deal with it. **Here is a quick action plan for dealing with these powerful forces:**

1 BE HONEST.

First John 1:8 makes it clear that "if we claim to be without sin, we deceive ourselves and the truth is not in us." In other words, we need to be honest with ourselves and others about our sins. I think that it is especially true when it comes to sexual sin. "Honesty" doesn't mean telling everyone details of your sins or temptations. It does mean admitting that sexual purity can be difficult. So many times I hear Christian teens who speak as though they never struggle with sexual sins. It's possible that some of them really don't struggle as much in this area. But I think for most teens the real reason is that admitting to a struggle on this issue is seen as "unspiritual." But to truly have victory one needs to first recognize that there is a battle and there is an enemy that all of us struggle with to one degree or another. Be honest with yourself and God about your personal struggle with sexual purity (and whatever other sins you may be struggling with, for that matter, like pride, gossip, envy, etc.). ✖

2 DEVELOP HOLY HABITS.

Holy habits are essential for holy living. What do I mean by that? It is not allowing anything to go through our minds that could cause us to stumble sexually. This means being careful as to what movie scenes we allow ourselves to watch and what music lyrics we allow ourselves to listen to, what Internet sites we allow ourselves to surf and what conversations we allow ourselves to have. It is being careful not to be in a position that might lead to sin, like being all alone in a house with someone you're dating. Every scene, song, site, or situation should go through the grid of this question: "Is this something that pleases God?" If not, turn it off, fast-forward it, or trash it. Just don't let it stain your brain. The mind is a terrible thing to waste.

But holy habits are not just saying no to the bad but yes to the good. This means getting in a regular regimen of studying God's Word and praying. Notice what I am not talking about . . . just reading the Bible. There is a big difference between reading God's Word and studying it. I know of a lot of Christian teenagers who read their Bibles every day and still don't have a clue. It's because they are reading and not studying. Ask yourself, What does this passage mean? What does it mean to me? How can I apply it right away? The more you study God's Word and get it, the more you have ammunition to fight against sin and Satan. As David wrote in Psalm 119:11, "I have hidden your word in my heart that I might not sin against you."

And don't underestimate the power of prayer in the battle for sexual purity. I am not talking about reciting the prayer of Jabez or the Lord's Prayer in some robotic fashion every night before bed. I am talking about getting real with God. I am talking about pouring out your heart to Him on a regular basis and telling Him your deepest, darkest sins and your hidden, secret struggles. Maybe that means journaling your prayers to God. That is a habit that I have been in since I was fifteen years old. (I am thirty-seven now. I know, I know . . . that's really old.) Since I was a teenager I have written out my prayers to God and journaled my journey in the battle for sexual purity and Christlike living. As I look back over the journals, I see the thrill of victory and the agony of defeat. Each time I read them I am reminded of the importance of developing holy habits from the time one is young. Believe me, it pays off when you get old like me.

3 TRUST IN GOD.

This is the single most important thing to remember in your battle for sexual purity as a young MIB. All the holy habits in the world cannot keep you from sexual sin. Ultimately it is only the power of the risen Christ that will guarantee you victory over sin. When Jesus died on the cross, the power of sin was broken. The power that raised Jesus from the dead is the same power that will raise us above the power of sin and temptation into victory. As we trust in His Spirit who dwells within us, that power kicks in and we are victorious. When we stop trusting in His power and look instead to ourselves, we are doomed to failure. The only hope that we have to be sexually pure over the long haul is rooted in our daily declaration of dependence on Jesus Christ and His finished work on the cross. ✠

Ephesians 6:10 calls us to "be strong in the Lord and in his mighty power." The enemy of lust is too big, too powerful, and too dangerous for us to defeat by ourselves. But when we are strong in the Lord, when we choose to trust in Him instead of ourselves, we are sure to be victorious. ✠

I come from a family of title-winning bodybuilders. My family is tough, big, and bad. I am not. I didn't need to be growing up. It was kind of like being in a mafia family. Nobody messed with me in my tough, inner-city neighborhood because our family was known around town for being big, bad, and, when need be, ruthlessly violent. The key was to stay close to home. The farther I got away from our house, the more dangerous it was. The closer I stayed to home, the less dangerous it was, because when I was close to home, I was close to my muscle-bound, tattooed, ready-for-a-fight family. When I was close to them, any thugs or gangsters would just keep driving by. ✠

The same is true with our relationship with Jesus Christ. The spiritual gangster called sexual sin can't mess with us when we stay close to our heavenly Father. As we trust in Him, commune with Him, obey Him, and stay right by His side, those sins will just keep driving by. But stray too far from His side and . . . well, nothing good happens. ✠

DEAL AND *HEAL*.

All of us need to learn how to deal with the sexual temptation that drives by every day. Many of us need to learn to heal from the sexual compromise that has hit us in the past. Have you blown it when it comes to purity? Are you scared and scarred by the guilt that comes hand in hand with sexual sin? There is hope in Jesus Christ. He is the One who forgives our sin, restores our souls, and cleanses our hearts. He is what I like to call "The Revirginizer." He cleanses us from our past sin and restores us to fellowship with Him. Oh, yes, the consequences are still there, but our pure relationship with God is restored. ❈

Jesus Christ is more than just the Savior of your soul. He is also the redeemer of your past. Paul wrote these awesome words in Philippians 3:13–14: "One thing I do: Forgetting what is behind and straining toward what is ahead, I press on toward the goal to win the prize for which God has called me heavenward in Christ Jesus." Forget the past and press on toward the goal to become like Jesus. One day He will wash away the memories of those disgusting sins of yesterday as you enter into eternity hand in hand with Him. Until then, through His grace, put the past behind and focus on the future. ❈

Here are a few more things to remember in your quest toward restoration:

4 CONFESS YOUR SIN TO GOD AND RECEIVE HIS FORGIVENESS.

"If we confess our sins, he is faithful and just and will forgive us our sins and purify us from all unrighteousness" (1 John 1:9). That is a promise. When you fess up that you messed up, He forgives and forgets. That awesome promise is for us as His children as we seek to live this thing called the Christian life but fail along the way. We can know that every single time we break His heart, when we turn to Him and tell Him that we sinned, restoration is promised. It doesn't matter how far you have fallen or how much you have sinned. Your relationship with God is fully restored when you fully confess to Him. ❇

Some of us have a hard time receiving that forgiveness for sexual sin. My mom did. You see, my mom had a past when it came to sexual sin. I am one of the unintended results of one of those relationships. For years I witnessed to my mom and she thought that God would never forgive her. But finally one day she understood the power of the Cross and received the forgiveness of God. ❇

Maybe you, like my mom, need to receive His forgiveness for sexual sin in your past. God tells us that when He forgives us He separates us from that sin as far as the east is from the west and casts that sin into the deepest ocean. It is gone. You are forgiven. Now you can walk in purity as a "revirginized" MIB for the glory of God. ❇

5   CONFESS YOUR SIN TO SOMEONE ELSE AND RECEIVE ACCOUNTABILITY.

James 5:16 reminds us to confess our sins "to each other and pray for each other so that you may be healed." This doesn't mean that we have to confess every sin to everyone. But you should have somebody whom you love and respect spiritually who knows everything (maybe your youth leader, a pastor at your church, or your parents). That person can pray for you and keep you accountable so that you can continue the healing process. ❖

6 REFUSE TO GIVE UP NO MATTER WHAT.

"For though a righteous man falls seven times, he rises again" (Proverbs 24:16). Have you fallen seven times? Seventy times? Seven hundred times? Get back up. Refuse to stay down in the muck of immorality for even a second. Keep "failing forward" and limping toward the finish line as God teaches you purity day after day and moment after moment. But remember this . . . the battle for sexual purity never ends in this life. It is like having a pet rattlesnake—as soon as you think it's tame, it bites you. Refuse to give up, give in, or give way to sexual sin. ❖

Will the real MIB please stand up? ❖

Move aside, Will Smith and Tommy Lee Jones. The real MIB are not protecting the earth from some alien invasion but from a satanic conspiracy. The real MIB aren't armed with high-powered weapons of super-charged destruction, but unstoppable spiritual weapons that destroy spiritual strongholds. The real MIB don't use tools that wipe out memories, but a message that wipes out sin. The real MIB have the mission to invade and persuade as they deal and heal. The real MIB are you and me. Will Smith ain't got nothing on us. ❖

Student Survival Tips

1. Get ready to invade and persuade. If you are going to reach your friends for Jesus Christ as a real MIB, then you must know how to share your faith effectively. Check out www.dare2share.org for free training resources that will help you share the gospel with your friends (and complete strangers!).

2. Learn how to deal with sexual temptation by getting a close friend who is passionate about Jesus to keep you accountable. Remember that you don't have to tell everyone about every sexual sin that you may be struggling with, but there should be at least one person (of your own sex) who knows everything and can keep you accountable.

3. Begin the process of healing from past sexual compromise. Tell your youth leader, counselor, parent, or pastor about it and begin the slow road to recovery. Remember that no matter what the scar, God can heal you whole in His perfect timing!

WORST-CASE SCENARIO

You have lost your virginity and don't feel like God can ever use you for His purposes. You feel guilty and unworthy. What do you do?

THE TRIBAL CHALLENGE

Ask God to help you pick a number (100, 500, 1000, whatever!) of students that you want to reach with the gospel message at your schools this year, and then brainstorm ten ways you can be MIB on your campuses to accomplish that goal!

Fear Factors

✠ OK, SO I LIKE TV REALITY SHOWS. *FEAR FACTOR* IS ONE OF THOSE SHOWS THAT GETS MY ATTENTION EVERY TIME—SIX CONTESTANTS WHO DARE TO FACE THEIR BIGGEST FEARS SO THEY CAN WIN THE BIG PRIZE OF $50,000.

FROM BALANCING CHALLENGES FAR ABOVE THE GROUND TO DEATH-DEFYING PLUNGES UNDERNEATH THE WATER, FROM EATING THE UNIMAGINABLE TO HAVING INSECTS, SPIDERS, RATS, AND SNAKES COVER THEIR BODIES, THESE SIX CONTESTANTS FACE THE MOST EMBARRASSING, THE MOST DARING, AND THE MOST DANGEROUS CHALLENGES IN ORDER TO WIN THE PRIZE. KIND OF SOUNDS LIKE SHARING YOUR FAITH IN THE END TIMES. 🁢

I am convinced that evangelism in the end times is the ultimate fear-factor challenge. As a matter of fact I personally believe that someday right here in America it will be against the law to actively share your faith. It will be seen as an invasion of privacy and a crude and rude act of intrusion. Even now it is difficult to bring up spiritual subjects in the mall, at work, or at school without facing some kind of legal or social repercussions. But that's OK. It was the same way in the book of Acts. Check this out:

hen they called them in again and commanded them not to speak or teach at all in the name of Jesus. But Peter and John replied, "Judge for yourselves whether it is right in God's sight to obey you rather than God. For we cannot help speaking about what we have seen and heard." (Acts 4:18–20)

Peter and John were commanded to shut up by the Sanhedrin (the Jewish ruling authorities of that day). This was the same group of men that engineered the crucifixion of Jesus Christ. Talk about fear factor! But Peter and John didn't flinch. They basically said, "We can't help it. We are going to obey God rather than you." They faced their fears and later suffered for it. ⊞

 hey called the apostles in and had them flogged. Then they ordered them not to speak in the name of Jesus, and let them go. The apostles left the Sanhedrin, rejoicing because they had been counted worthy of suffering disgrace for the Name. Day after day, in the temple courts and from house to house, they never stopped teaching and proclaiming the good news that Jesus is the Christ. (Acts 5:40–42)

Even after they were beaten with a whip these guys wouldn't shut up! They couldn't shut up. You see, the faith factor in their hearts was greater than any fear factor that they faced! The same can be true with you and me when it comes to sharing our faith in the end times. ⊞

So what are some of those fear factors that you must face when sharing your faith? What are the biggest challenges that you must overcome if you are going to be a powerful witness for Jesus Christ in the end times? I believe there are at least four.

FEAR FACTOR #1
What will my friends say about me?

FEAR FACTOR #2
What if I don't know what to say?

FEAR FACTOR #3
What if somebody asks me a question that I can't answer?

FEAR FACTOR #4
I'm not sure myself that I am going to heaven!

Let's face each of these fear factors head-on and win the ultimate prize of seeing people put their faith and trust in Jesus Christ!

FEAR FACTOR #1
WHAT WILL MY FRIENDS SAY ABOUT ME?

As I travel with Dare 2 Share Ministries across the country and train tens of thousands of teenagers to share their faith, I talk to them about their biggest fears when it comes to witnessing. Again and again the answer that comes up the most is fear of what their friends will think about them. ✖

And let's be honest, that is a risk. When you share the gospel with a stranger, you have nothing to lose. When you share the gospel with a friend, the friendship itself could be at risk. ✖

So why in the world should you take that risk? I will give you two reasons: Realize whose you are and what's at stake. ✖

REALIZE WHOSE YOU ARE

Paul the apostle lost a lot of friends for sharing the gospel. So why did he continue to do it? Because he found his identity in pleasing his master . . . the Lord

Jesus Christ. Listen to what he wrote in Galatians 1:10: "Am I now trying to win the approval of men, or of God? Or am I trying to please men? If I were still trying to please men, I would not be a servant of Christ." 🈸

Ultimately Paul knew that if he tried to make all of his friends happy, then he would break God's heart. And if he tried to make God happy by sharing the gospel, he could lose many of his friends. That was a risk he was willing to take because he found his identity in what God thought of him and not in what others thought of him. 🈸

That is why it is so important that you grow deep in your relationship with God on a moment-by-moment basis. As you fall in love with Him, pleasing Him becomes more important to you than anything else. Pleasing Him becomes your biggest passion. What others think about you and your Christianity begins to dissolve away. 🈸

REALIZE WHAT'S AT STAKE

Stop and think about the gruesome reality for your friends if they don't put their faith and trust in Jesus Christ. They could face the coming Tribulation without rescue. They will face the flames of an eternal hell without end. And they face their own daily struggles without hope. Their very souls are at stake without Jesus Christ. 🈸

Stop for a moment and think about what it would be like if your best friend had cancer. In the early stages your friend receives chemotherapy and radiation and all of the medical treatment possible . . . to no avail. As you watch your friend shrivel away to nothing but skin and bone as the cancer devours every cell of his or her body, you are brokenhearted. Then one day, through some strange turn of events, you accidentally stumble across the cure for your friend's form of cancer. What do you do? Do you keep the cure to yourself for fear of losing or offending your friend? Do you keep silent because you are too busy with other things to share the cure? Do you just keep living your normal life? No! Of course not! ❖

If your best friend had cancer and you found the cure, you would rush to the person's side right away and give the person the cure so that his or her body could be completely healed! Not only that, but you would tell all of the doctors and nurses you could find. You would go to all the hospitals in your city and tell the good news. Soon you would be traveling the world, doing every television interview and radio interview you possibly could, shouting out the good news to anyone who would listen that you had the cure to cancer! Right? You wouldn't be worried at all about what your friends or anybody else thought of you, because you had a message that had to be shared with the world! Right? ❖

Well, you and I have the cure to something much more devastating and terminal than cancer. We have the cure to a wasted life and a torturous eternity. We have the cure to depression and discouragement. We have the cure to broken families and shattered relationships. We have the cure to sin and to hell . . . the gospel of Jesus Christ. As bad and as devastating as the effects of cancer are to the body, they pale in comparison to the effects of sin on the soul. Sin "cells" rage against the heart, eat away at the conscience, infect the brain, contaminate the soul, and kill the spirit of humanity. But sin's consequences don't stop when we die . . . they begin. An eternity in a blazing inferno of hell and hopelessness lies in wait after the final beat of a person's heart reverberates. If we could see into the souls of strangers and friends and family without Jesus, we would see something worse than any cancer anywhere has done to anyone. ❖

Right now my mom is dying of cancer. She has been smoking for fifty-two years and has a large tumor in her lung. That cancer has spread to her back and rib and arm. As I type these words, she is recovering from the devastating chemo treatments that are raging against the cancer cells in her body. We don't know how long she has to live, and it is breaking my heart to see her suffer like this. If I had the cure I would share it with my mom (and everybody else I could find) as quickly as possible. ❖

I think one of the problems with a lot of Christian teens (and adults for that matter) when it comes to sharing their faith is that they have forgotten what is at stake. I also am convinced that many are more concerned about being cool than being witnesses for Jesus. The problem is that it is going to be one or the other. If we are truly sharing our faith, then here is what Jesus says will happen: "All men will hate you because of me. . . . A student is not above his teacher, nor a servant above his master. . . . If the head of the house has been called Beelzebub, how much more the members of his household! So do not be afraid of them" (Matthew 10:22, 24–26).

The Bible also says in 1 Corinthians 1:18, "For the message of the cross is foolishness to those who are perishing, but to us who are being saved it is the power of God." Those who reject Christ think the gospel message is stupid! So the question is, Are you willing to look stupid and share your faith? Are you willing to become uncool to share the gospel with those in your life? Are you willing to lose your friends so that they can hear the only message that can save them?

Be loving, be kind, be wise, be persuasive, but be sharing . . . their souls are at stake. The cancer of sin must be stopped even if we lose our "cool" as a result.

Someday, at the judgment seat of Christ, when we stand and give account for our lives before the Lord Jesus Christ, there will be a lot of regret. We will see in a flash all the wasted time due to sin and self, all of the glory that we could have brought to Christ but didn't, and all of the missed opportunities to share Jesus. On that day the saddest words we could utter are "if only."

"IF ONLY"

David's on the football team;
He plays so very hard.
School is not so much his thing,
But he likes to party hard.

Ashley is a cheerleader;
She works hard every practice.
David is her boyfriend.
He fits her social status.

David is my best friend;
I date his sister Sue.
I've known them all since second grade.
We've been great friends right on through.

Now I sit 'midst broken glass.
His blood upon my clothes.
Ashley lies beside him
Upon the gravel road.

Sue, she's dying in my arms—
She cannot hear me scream.
My voice hurts from yelling
And calling out her name.

A shortcut to the football field,
A few too many beers,
A sharp turn of the country road,
And now I sit in tears.

IF ONLY I would have told them,
IF ONLY I would have shared.
I thought they wouldn't listen;
I thought they wouldn't care.

They'd be going to heaven's glory
Instead of hell's hot flames,
If only I would have witnessed
And quit playing little, stupid games.

So learn from my sad story.
Don't miss out on God's plan;
Life is short and dangerous—
Share Christ while you can.

FEAR FACTOR #2
WHAT IF I DON'T KNOW
WHAT TO SAY?

This is another big, big fear that many teens (and adults) have when it comes to sharing the gospel of Jesus Christ. I am absolutely convinced that down deep inside most Christian teenagers want to share the gospel, but they just don't know how. How do you bring it up? How do you spell it out? How do you wrap it up? These questions and more all rattle around in our brains and become gigantic excuses for us to keep our mouths shut when it comes to witnessing to our friends. ▓

In the next few chapters you are going to learn what to say. Just realize this one powerful truth—sharing the gospel message is easier than you think. It is a story . . . a story that just happens to be true. It is the message that God loved us so much that He sent His only Son to die in our place for all of our sins and that through simple faith in Him we can enter into a personal, permanent relationship with the God of the universe. ▓

As you read this book you will learn a practical technique to bringing it up, spelling it out, and wrapping it up called "The 2.6.2 Technique." But the bottom line is this: The message of the gospel is amazingly simple and unique. Don't be intimidated. You don't need to hold a degree in theology to tell it. As a matter of fact, most people in the Bible who shared the message were simple people like you and me who couldn't help but bring it up and spell it out to everyone around them. ✥

FEAR FACTOR #3
WHAT IF SOMEBODY ASKS ME A QUESTION THAT I CAN'T ANSWER?

Stumped. I hate that word. I hate being stumped in an area of trivia (specifically movies and Bible trivia). I hate being stumped by a crossword puzzle (that's why I refuse to do them). I hate being stumped in general. You probably do too. It's the fear of being stumped that keeps a lot of Christian teenagers from sharing their faith. They think to themselves, *Somebody's going to ask me some question and I am not going to have the answer for it, and then I am going to look like an idiot.* But this is just one way of looking at it. ✥

I look at getting stumped while witnessing as a learning opportunity. As the old saying goes, "Fool me once, shame on you. Fool me twice, shame on me." My rule of thumb is this: You can fool me once with a question but never twice with the same question. Why? Because somebody taught me the secret of never getting burned twice with the same question when I was a teenager. I call it "the argument buster." It goes like this. Somebody asks you a question that you don't have the answer to, so you use the argument buster: "I don't know. But I'll find out." You then go back and study the Bible. Maybe you call your youth pastor and he or she doesn't know, so the youth pastor calls the senior pastor, and still no luck. Your senior pastor finally calls his old seminary teacher and, finally, the answer comes back. You take the answer back to the person who asked you the question, and you present the person with a solid, biblical answer . . . an answer that you will never forget. Sometimes you may have to say, "I looked for an answer, and to be honest I still don't know. But here are some possibilities." ▓

The great thing about using the argument buster is that after a while all of the questions start sounding the same. And pretty soon you have a well-reasoned arsenal of answers that you have learned by using this simple statement of honesty. ▓

Another benefit is that it continues the conversation. You may have to tell the person that you are witnessing to, "That's a great question. I have no idea what the answer is, but I will find out. Let's get together again next week and talk about it." ▓

I think that the beauty of the argument buster is that it is blatantly honest. Too many times we as Christians pretend we have all of the answers. As a result we are perceived (sometimes rightfully so) as arrogant people who are not willing to dialogue. We

don't have all of the answers. But we know the One who
does . . . Jesus Christ. Our mission is to introduce people
to the Person who can ultimately answer all of their
questions through His Word and Spirit. ❖

FEAR FACTOR #4
I'M NOT SURE MYSELF THAT
I AM GOING TO HEAVEN!

You may be thinking to yourself, *Well, that's all fine
and good about sharing my faith, but I am not so sure
that I will be going to heaven when I die. How can I
share the gospel if I am not exactly sure myself?* Good
question. But before I attempt to give you an answer, let
me share a few things with you. ❖

YOU ARE NOT ALONE

According to George Barna (a guy who studies
things like this), half of the teenagers in America who
are currently attending youth group are not Christians
themselves. That's about seven million teens who go to
church week in and week out, but don't know for sure
that they are going to heaven as a result of a personal
relationship with Jesus Christ. So don't freak out. You
are not alone. ❖

IT'S A SIMPLE MESSAGE

I know. I know. I have said it before. But it's worth repeating. Knowing where you're going after you die is not a complicated matter. It's a matter of simple faith in Jesus Christ. ▒

So here it goes. Here is the gospel story. ▒

Thousands of years ago, God made humanity to be in fellowship with Him. But we blew it. We sinned. We broke His commands (and His heart). That sin became a barrier between us and God. Although He loved us, He hated our sin. He hated that sin so much and loved us so much that two thousand years ago He sent His only Son into the world. Jesus Christ lived a perfect life and then died a horrible death . . . on purpose. He was born to die for you and for me. He suffered in our place for our sin. He took God's punishment for sin on our behalf. He died for every sin you and I have ever committed or will commit. All we must do is believe that He died for us and trust in Him alone to take us to heaven and forgive us our sins, and we receive the free gift of eternal life. ▒

That's right, I said "receive," not "achieve." You see, most people think that going to heaven is something that is achieved. If you live a good enough life, they say, God will let you into His glorious presence. No way. God would never let us into His perfect heaven in our sinful condition. And any number of good deeds we do could never erase the stain of sin from our souls. But when we believe that Jesus died for us and trust in Him alone to forgive us our sins, we receive the free gift of eternal life. This thing called eternal life is a personal and permanent relationship that can never be broken by us and will never be broken by God. �

Jesus put it this way in John 3:16, "For God so loved the world that he gave his one and only Son, that who-ever believes in him shall not perish but have eternal life." That's it. You believe and you receive the free gift of God. ✖

If you don't know for sure that you are going to heaven when you die, you can know before you finish reading this chapter. All you must do is trust in Jesus and what He did for you on the cross to forgive you for all of your sins. When you do that, you are saved from the power and penalty of sin forever. ✖

You can say this simple prayer in your mind right now if you are trusting in Him. Just remember that say-ing a prayer never saved anybody. It's your faith in Jesus Christ that saves you. Saying a prayer is simply a way of expressing your faith to God and thanking Him for the gift He has given you. Repeat these words to God:

"Dear God, right now I believe that Jesus died for all of my sins. I am trusting in Him and Him alone to forgive me for all of my sins. I receive your free gift of eternal life right now. Thank You so much for Your awesome gift to me. Amen." ✖

Write this date down. *"Today on* _____

I, _____, *put my faith and trust in*

Jesus Christ. This is a day I will never forget because on

this day I received the free gift of eternal life."

And now that you are a Christian you will never, ever have to worry about the ultimate fear factor . . . the fear of death. Check these verses out in Hebrews 2:14–15 (emphasis mine): "Since the children [that's us] have flesh and blood, he [Jesus Christ] too shared in their humanity so **that by his death he might destroy him who holds the power of death—that is, the devil—and free those who all their lives were held in slavery by their fear of death.**" Did you get that? Jesus Himself faced the final fear-factor challenge on our behalf. He faced Satan himself and destroyed his power completely when He died on the cross. As a result we no longer have to fear death. When Jesus died He crushed not only sin and Satan but the fear of death. �֍

All of the fear factors that we face are ultimately answered in Jesus Christ. Our fear of what our friends may think of us is answered in finding our security in what Jesus thinks of us. Our fear of not knowing what to say is rooted in understanding the simple message of Jesus Christ. Our fear of not having the right answer when somebody asks us a question is found in knowing the Book that Jesus Christ inspired. Our fear of not going to heaven is erased when we believe that Jesus died for us. ✖

You see, one thing is greater than all of the fear factors combined . . . the faith factor. When we trust in Him, game over. We win. ✖

STUDENT SURVIVAL TIPS

1. Facing your fears when it comes to sharing your faith is a team sport. Get a few friends at school who are just as determined to reach out to those who don't know Christ. Pray for and encourage each other!

2. Learn more about how to share your faith by attending a training event for teenagers (like a Dare 2 Share conference).

3. Grow deep in your own personal knowledge of God's Word. The more you know, the more you are able to share and, when necessary, defend the message of Jesus. Spend time every day reading the Bible and asking God through His Spirit to help you understand your faith more.

4. Find your identity in Christ! The more you build your relationship with Jesus through prayer, the less you care about what others may say about you when you share your faith. Let your love for Jesus consume you to the point that you don't care what others think of you and your Christianity!

Worst-Case-Scenario

You are sharing your faith at school during a break between classes when a teacher approaches you and tells you that it is illegal for you to "proselytize" at school because of "separation of church and state" issues. You are sent to the principal's office where you are threatened with possible expulsion if you continue to share your faith. What do you do? (Hint: The boldness of a lion and gentleness of a lamb should define a serious follower of Jesus in all volatile situations. By the way, it's not illegal.)

The Tribal Challenge

Go to a local shopping mall on a busy day and don't witness to anyone for thirty minutes. Each of you separate and sit in different parts of the mall for thirty minutes. As you watch people walk by, imagine a tag on their foreheads that reads "Bound for hell." Imagine those people burning in the flames of hell forever without hope. Write your thoughts down as you imagine them in eternal fire and pain. Get together with everyone afterward and compare notes. Spend time in prayer for the lost, asking God to break your hearts for those who don't know Jesus. Then, if you have an opportunity to witness, go for it!

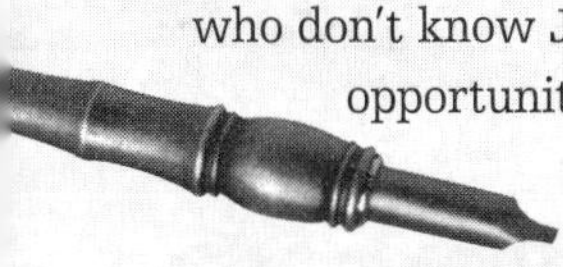

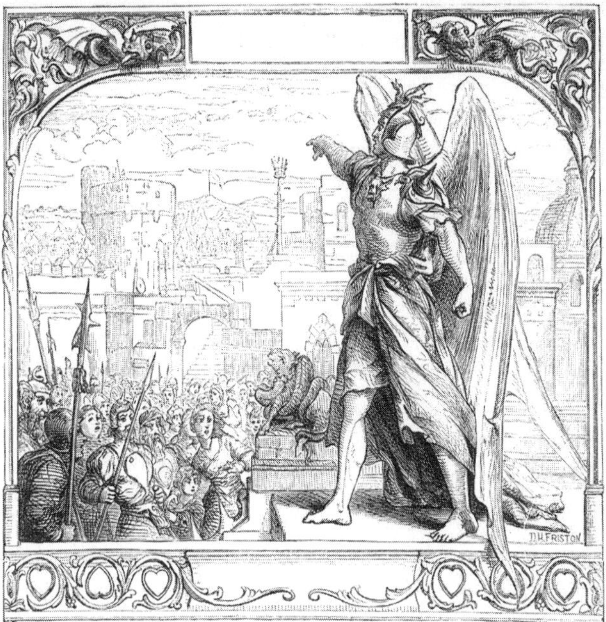

4

An End-Times Evangelism Survival Kit

I will never forget Natalie. She was selling movie tickets at a theater in Lincoln, Nebraska. I got into Lincoln in

THE LATE AFTERNOON TO PREPARE FOR AN UPCOMING DARE 2 SHARE CONFERENCE. THE NEXT DAY I WAS GOING TO DO A PROMOTIONAL LUNCHEON FOR YOUTH LEADERS IN THE LINCOLN AREA, BUT I HAD A LITTLE BIT OF TIME ON MY HANDS, AND I DECIDED TO GO TO A MOVIE. THAT'S WHERE I MET NATALIE. ❖

The movie theater was kind of dead that night. And I noticed as I purchased my ticket that she was reading a book. As I looked closer I saw that it was one of the "Left Behind" books. So after I introduced myself to her I took the opportunity to strike up a conversation. It went something like this . . .

"So you are reading one of the 'Left Behind' books," I commented.

"Yeah," she responded politely.

"I hear they are going to make a movie out of it or something," I said.

"Really?"

"Yeah."

"So what do you think about the book?" I asked again.

"It's good, but it kind of scares me."

"Why does it scare you?" I probed deeper.

"Well, because I don't want to go through the Tribulation!" she exclaimed.

"Natalie, a lot of Christians believe the Bible says that if you are a Christian you won't go through the Tribulation. So, if they're right, you don't have to be afraid if you are a Christian."

"That's the problem. I don't know for sure if I am a Christian or not," she said.

"If I could tell you in just a few minutes how you could know that you were a Christian, would that be good news?" I asked.

"Yes, I don't want to go through the Tribulation. I want to go to heaven."

Over the next few minutes Natalie trusted in Jesus Christ, right there behind the ticket counter at the movie theater in Lincoln, Nebraska. She came to the Dare 2 Share conference a few months later and learned to spread the good news to others. It was an awesome experience. And it wasn't hard at all. Why? Because we are living in a culture where it is easy to bring up spiritual subjects. ✄

RECOGNIZE THAT SPIRITUALITY IS COOL . . . CHRISTIANITY IS NOT

Go into any Barnes and Noble or Borders and look around. You will see spiritual topics everywhere. You will see the Harry Potter version of spirituality in the children's section. In the fiction section you will see the Star Wars version of spirituality ("the Force," of course). You'll see Yoga spirituality in the health and fitness section. As a matter of fact, no matter what section you are in you will find something spiritual. Why? Because we live in a culture that is extremely spiritual. Spirituality is hip. Buddhism and Scientology have taken Hollywood by storm. The subject of religion is no longer taboo. ✄

That gives us, as Christians, a great opportunity. Because we live in a culture that is spiritually inclined, it is easy to bring up spiritual subjects. You can easily turn most conversations toward the spiritual. This makes it easier on one level to witness to your friends. �

After the events of 9-11 it became even easier to bring up the subject. Suddenly, people are not just talking about spirituality but life and death and heaven and hell. I remember sitting in a Starbucks when a group of high school girls came in and sat down in a big circle of eight. They were all talking about the terrorist attacks in America, and one was leading the conversation. At first I thought that she was a Christian girl who was skillfully weaving the conversation toward the message of the gospel. But then she proclaimed, "I was an atheist before 9-11. But now I am rethinking everything I ever believed about God. All this stuff has got me thinking." She was bringing it up all on her own and the rest of the girls were joining in. Nobody was offended. Why? Because spirituality is cool. ✻

The problem is that true Christianity is not cool. Don't misunderstand what I am saying. I think Christianity is the most awesome message ever to hit planet Earth. But there is a big, big difference between spirituality and Christianity. For one, spirituality is inclusive and Christianity is exclusive. In other words, spirituality welcomes all beliefs and all religions as equally valid and true. Christianity doesn't. Jesus Himself said, "I am the way and the truth and the life. No one comes to the Father except through me" (John 14:6). That's pretty exclusive. Spirituality says, "All paths lead to God." Christianity says, "One path leads to God . . . Jesus Christ and Him alone." ✻

So, one of the benefits of sharing the gospel in this

culture is that it is easy to bring up as a spiritual topic. But it gets tougher when you get to the punch line of your message . . . Jesus is the only way to heaven.

Second, spirituality is generally based on some good things that you do to earn God's favor or get to heaven or get reincarnated as something better or whatever. Christianity is not based on what we do. It is based on what Christ has done. We don't achieve it. We receive it. It has nothing to do with us and everything to do with Jesus Christ. Ephesians 2:8–9 puts it this way, "For it is by grace you have been saved, through faith—and this not from yourselves, it is the gift of God—not by works, so that no one can boast." Spirituality says that you earn it by giving more, chanting more, sacrificing more, or whatever. Christianity says you do nothing but receive it through simple faith. We have nothing to brag about. Because in the long run all we did was to believe in what Jesus did.

Finally, Satan will do everything he can to get teenagers to be spiritual and reject Jesus Christ as the only way to heaven. Second Corinthians 4:4 puts it this way, "The god of this age [Satan] has blinded the minds of unbelievers, so that they cannot see the light of the gospel of the glory of Christ, who is the image of God." Satan will do everything he can to keep the eyes of the unbeliever blinded to the truth of the gospel of Jesus. Distracting a person with spirituality is one of his favorite tactics.

Thinking of false teachers who speak about "spirituality" but not real Christianity, listen to what God says. "For such men are false apostles, deceitful work-

men, masquerading as apostles of Christ. And no wonder, for Satan himself masquerades as an angel of light.
It is not surprising, then, if his servants masquerade as
servants of righteousness. Their end will be what their
actions deserve" (2 Corinthians 11:13–15). ✄

ASSEMBLE THE SURVIVAL KIT

This is why you need an End-Times Evangelism
Survival Kit. You need some basic tools to help you share
your faith in a culture where spirituality is cool but
true Christianity is not. This kit is not complicated. As
a matter of fact, there are only four items in it . . . the
gospel message, a thing called "witnessing radar," a
funnel, and a simple test. That is it. These four tools will
help you share your faith effectively in a way that fits
your style in a culture that just doesn't get it when it
comes to Jesus. ✄

THE GOSPEL

This is the most important tool that you have in
your survival kit. If you could only grab one thing out of
the kit, you should grab this essential tool. What is it? It
is the unstoppable message that Christ died for our sins
and rose again, and that through simple faith in Him we
can have hope on earth now and eternity in heaven
someday. According to Romans 1:16, the gospel is "the
power of God." This message is like a grenade that blows
a person out of the kingdom of darkness and into the
kingdom of God. It is like a cure that heals the shredded

hearts and souls of humanity who have been devastated by the effects of sin and Satan. It is like a blanket to keep you warm in a cold world. It is like a rock to build your house upon. It is unlike any message or philosophy or belief system or religion you have ever heard or will ever be exposed to. 🎴

This tool is like a Swiss Army Knife. It does much more than one thing! It saves the soul, heals the heart, stretches the mind, soothes the conscience, erases guilt, and repels the devil. We will spend much more time on understanding the gospel message in the next chapter. In the meantime, just know that in the battle for souls the gospel message told in the power of the Spirit is your most powerful weapon on earth and the most important tool in your kit! 🎴

WITNESSING RADAR

The next tool in your kit is what I call "witnessing radar." It is the skill of learning how to turn conversations toward spiritual things and then toward Jesus Christ. It is learning how to bring up Jesus naturally in the course of everyday conversations. I use the word *skill* because that's exactly what it is. It takes practice, work, and discipline over the long haul. I have been sharing my faith actively for twenty-five years, and it is a skill I am still working to improve. Let me give you a great example of witnessing radar. It is found in the book of Acts, chapter 17. Paul was in Athens witnessing to the Greek philosophers on Mars Hill, and he used his witnessing radar to bring the gospel up naturally. Check it out . . .

group of Epicurean and Stoic philosophers began to dispute with him. Some of them asked, "What is this babbler trying to say?" Others remarked, "He seems to be advocating foreign gods." They said this because Paul was preaching the good news about Jesus and the resurrection. Then they took him and brought him to a meeting of the Areopagus, where they said to him, "May we know what this new teaching is that you are presenting? You are bringing some strange ideas to our ears, and we want to know what they mean." (All the Athenians and the foreigners who lived there spent their time doing nothing but talking about and listening to the latest ideas.) Paul then stood up in the meeting of the Areopagus and said: "Men of Athens! I see that in every way you are very religious. For as I walked around and looked carefully at your objects of worship, I even found an altar with this inscription: TO AN UNKNOWN GOD. Now what you worship as something unknown I am going to proclaim to you." (Acts 17:18–23)

Earlier in the day Paul was checking out the countless altars spread all around Athens. And, bam, he found one with the inscription "to an unknown god" and used his witnessing radar. He thought to himself, *This will be a great way to bring up the gospel naturally to the people of Athens.* ✠

How do you sharpen your skills when it comes to your witnessing radar? Practice as a tribe (youth group, campus ministry, friends) picking subjects that have nothing to do with the gospel and turning that into a conversation that naturally turns toward spiritual subjects. The better you get at this skill, the easier it is and the more natural it is to share your faith. ✼

I will never forget being at the mall for a Corvette show. High-powered, chromed-out Corvettes were all over the place. One in particular caught my attention. It was black and beautiful. As I stood there in awe I noticed a guy standing next to me (engaging my witnessing radar). We struck up a conversation about the awesome car in front of us (a blip on the radar screen). "How fast do you think this car goes?" I asked.

"One hundred and forty-five miles per hour . . . easy" was his response.

"Can you imagine what it would be like to get in a car wreck going that fast?" I asked again.

"You would be dead" (radar fully engaged).

"That would be cool, because then I would be in heaven," I said.

It was quiet for a few seconds. Then he asked the inevitable question, "How do you know for sure that you would be in heaven?"

"You don't want to know" was my quick response.

"Yes, I do!" he demanded. This guy was begging me to give him the gospel, so I did! ✼

Not every witnessing experience goes quite that smoothly, but the point is this: The more you have your witnessing radar fully engaged, the easier it is to share your faith naturally. Be constantly on the lookout for how to turn conversations toward Christ. Colossians 4:5 commands us to "make the most of every opportunity" when it comes to sharing our faith. That means to consistently be on the lookout and to always have our witnessing radar fully engaged. ✼

THE FUNNEL
....

The funnel is the third tool in your survival kit. Having a funnel in a survival kit may sound weird, but think of sharing your faith as being something like trying to get a conversation into a funnel. A funnel is big on the top and narrow on the bottom. It's easy to get stuff into the top of a funnel because the top is big and round and open. Where it gets tricky is getting through the narrow bottom part of the funnel, which we'll call the spout. When sharing our faith our goal should be to get the talk to enter the funnel of "spirituality." The challenge is in getting the conversation down the spout . . . the narrow path . . . Jesus Christ. �֍

We live in a culture that is very open to spiritual things but not very open to true Christianity. Because of that it is easy to talk to our friends (or even strangers for that matter) about spiritual subjects (the top of the funnel), but when we get down to the fact that Jesus is the only way to heaven (the spout), it becomes more difficult. ✖

Remember what Jesus said in Matthew 7:13–14: "Enter through the narrow gate. For wide is the gate and broad is the road that leads to destruction, and many enter through it. But small is the gate and narrow the road that leads to life, and only a few find it." The broad way is spirituality and religion. The narrow way is Jesus Christ. Helping people find the narrow way, the bottom of the funnel, takes skill, wisdom, prayer, and God's help. ✖

THE TEST
....

Understanding the funnel and witnessing radar is just part of it. The next essential step is understanding your personal style of sharing your faith. Just like snowflakes, no two witnesses are exactly the same. But there are some general categories of "soul winners" that you probably fit into. ✲

I thank God for giving me the wife that He did. Although we are absolutely opposite, God has used (and is still using) our differences to balance us both. ✲

One of the areas that we are really different from each other in is the way that we share our faith. Debbie is much more relational than I am. She loves to cultivate conversations and turn them toward Christ at the right time. She is so nice that people deeply respect her, and so, although she doesn't witness to thousands of people every year, the ones she does share the gospel with take her very seriously. ✲

God has wired me to be much more direct and straightforward when it comes to sharing my faith. Whether it be on a plane or in a mall or at a movie theater, I love to engage people directly with the gospel message. Now don't get me wrong—I don't just go up to strangers and blast them right away with the gospel. Usually I get to know them for a few minutes and then steer the conversation down the "funnel," so to speak. It's the way I have always found success in sharing my faith. ✲

So the question is, which style is better, Debbie's or mine? The answer is neither . . . and both. God has so uniquely designed our witnessing wiring that each of us can find success in the way God has called us to share

His message. Your style is just as unique and powerful. So I ask you the question, "What's your witnessing style?" ✖

Begin the process of honestly looking inside yourself. What is your personality type? Are you shy and quiet or loud and "obnoxious"? Are you funny or serious? Are you introverted or extroverted? What about your spiritual gifting? Are you more of a listener or a talker? All of these questions and more will help you determine your spiritual bent when it comes to evangelism. You must know yourself if you are going to know your style. ✖

You don't have to be a Billy Graham or an apostle Paul to be effective at sharing your faith. You have to be you. ✖

TAKE THE TEST

This simple test will help you discover your own personal style of evangelism. Circle whichever answer describes you the most.

1. WHICH WORD DESCRIBES YOU THE BEST?

a. creative
b. bold
c. organized
d. caring

2. "SOMETIMES I TEND TO . . .

a. set my goals too high."
b. hurt people's feelings with my directness."
c. get impatient when things don't go as planned."

d. worry about what other people think of me."

3. WHICH PHRASE DESCRIBES YOU THE MOST?

a. To dream the impossible dream
b. Just do it!
c. A place for everything and everything in its place
d. Friends are friends forever

4. "MY FRIENDS WOULD PROBABLY DESCRIBE ME AS . . .

a. the life of the party."
b. the leader of the pack."
c. the smartest person they know."
d. a friend who really listens."

5. IF THERE WERE A FRIEND YOU WANTED TO LEAD TO CHRIST, WHICH OF THE FOLLOWING THINGS WOULD YOU BE MORE LIKELY TO DO?

a. Find the most creative way you possibly could to bring up the subject.
b. Just go and tell the person the gospel.
c. Think through all of the arguments that the person may have beforehand and then make a plan to initiate a well-thought-through presentation of the gospel.
d. Take the person out to a coffee shop and pray that it naturally comes up in the conversation.

6. WHAT MAKES YOU THE MOST UNCOMFORTABLE IN A WITNESSING SITUATION?

a. Not being able to reach the person right away in a creative way
b. Beating around the bush
c. Not knowing exactly what to say
d. Making the person you are witnessing to feel uncomfortable

7. WHAT IS YOUR BIGGEST CONCERN WHEN IT COMES TO EVANGELISM?

a. Boring the person
b. Being quiet about the gospel
c. Not being ready to share your faith logically
d. The other person's feelings

8. IF YOU WERE TO DESCRIBE YOUR WITNESSING STYLE, WHAT PHRASE WOULD YOU USE?

a. Unique, creative, and different!
b. Ready, willing, and able!
c. Always be prepared!
d. Earn the right to be heard!

9. "SOMETIMES I TEND TO BE . . .

a. idealistic when it comes to sharing my faith."
b. insensitive when it comes to sharing my faith."

c. impatient when it comes to sharing my faith."
d. intimidated when it comes to sharing my faith."

10. "IF I WERE TRYING TO MOTIVATE SOMEONE ELSE TO SHARE HIS FAITH, I WOULD TRY TO . . .

a. excite him about the impact he could make."
b. take him out witnessing."
c. help him know what he believes first."
d. encourage him to build strong relationships with the lost first."

So what are you? Mostly As, Bs, Cs, or Ds?

If you are mostly As, you are . . .

A VISION-DRIVEN EVANGELIST

Vision-driven evangelists are creative and innovative when it comes to evangelism because they see the big picture. Their goal is to have a maximum impact on those around them. To do this they let their imaginations run wild and are very strategic in their approach to leading others to Jesus Christ.

If you are mostly Bs, you are . . .

AN ACTION-DRIVEN EVANGELIST

Action-driven evangelists like to talk a lot. They are extremely outgoing and upbeat. These evangelism extroverts have no problem initiating conversations about the gospel with complete strangers. They ooze evangelism. Action-driven evangelists can't help telling others the good news of Jesus Christ. They love to introduce others to Him with a direct, verbal approach.

If you are mostly Cs, you are . . .

A LOGIC-DRIVEN EVANGELIST

Logic-driven evangelists are detailed, intellectual planners. They love to share their faith through healthy debate and well-thought-out discussions. They usually know their stuff and tend to be ready when it comes to objections. The best apologists (those who defend the faith with well-reasoned arguments) tend to be logic-driven evangelists.

If you are mostly Ds, you are . . .

A FRIENDSHIP-DRIVEN EVANGELIST

Friendship-driven evangelists are relational in their approach. They build bridges of love and kindness and then cross each bridge with the cargo of the gospel in a personal and sensitive way. Friendship-driven evangelists are usually great disciplers. Once they lead someone to Christ, the relationship is so strong already that getting that person out to church, youth group, or small group is usually not that much of a challenge.

UNDERSTAND YOUR MODEL

Each style of evangelism has a corresponding biblical model. As a matter of fact, I discovered these styles of evangelism by doing a study of the New Testament, grouping different types of witnesses into general categories. After narrowing these groups down again and again, I finally came to the four categories of vision-driven, action-driven, logic-driven, and friendship-driven evangelists. Finally, I picked one biblical character who represents that particular style of evangelism. 🕀

VISION-DRIVEN

The apostle Paul was a vision-driven evangelist. His slogan could have been "Win the world!" As made clear in Colossians 1:28, his goals for the gospel were high. He wanted to reach "everyone" with the gospel message and would not rest until "everyone" was saved and matured in Christ. His primary concern was maximum impact when it came to evangelism. He went to the biggest towns of that culture to make sure that he was being used by God to reach as many as possible. He also made it clear that he wanted new turf where the gospel had not been proclaimed. He wanted new soil to plant the seed of truth deeply. Paul was also extremely creative in the way he communicated the gospel of Jesus Christ. 🕀

ACTION-DRIVEN

Peter was action-driven. He was the first one to speak up and the last one to shut up. If he had a motto it could have been "Win the world . . . now!" He was extremely aggressive in his evangelism style. As evidenced by Acts 2 it is obvious that he didn't hesitate when he had an opportunity to deliver the gospel to an unreached audience. In Acts 2 a crowd of interested Jews gathered to hear the initial handful of believers speak in different languages simultaneously. Some thought they were drunk. Others probably thought they were just plain nuts. Peter seized the opportunity, jumped to his feet, and snagged the attention of the crowd of thousands: "Fellow Jews and all of you who are in Jerusalem, let me explain this to you; listen carefully to what I say. These men are not drunk, as you suppose. It's only nine in the morning! No, this is what was spoken by the prophet Joel" (vv. 14–16). In just seconds he seized their attention and transitioned into the gospel. In just minutes he had led three thousand people to Christ.

LOGIC-DRIVEN

Luke was logic-driven . . . by his own admission. Listen to the words he wrote to Theophilus.

> *Many have undertaken to draw up an account of the things that have been fulfilled among us, just as they were handed down to us by those who from the first were eyewitnesses and servants of the word. Therefore, since I myself have carefully investigated everything from the beginning, it seemed good also to me to write an orderly account for you, most excellent Theophilus, so that you may know the certainty of the things you have been taught.* (Luke 1:1–4)

Luke took more of an intellectual approach to evangelism. He, as a doctor, thought analytically and scientifically. He presented the message of hope in light of eyewitness accounts and hard-hitting evidence. Logic-driven evangelists tend to take a more analytical, intellectual approach to evangelism. They think their presentation through and share the gospel with their audiences persuasively and logically. They organize their message in such a way as to best appeal to the minds of those they are witnessing to. ✳

FRIENDSHIP-DRIVEN

Priscilla and Aquilla were friendship-driven in their witnessing style. In Acts 18 they met an impressive man named Apollos. "He was a learned man, with a thorough knowledge of the Scriptures" (v. 24). One problem, though—he hadn't yet heard of the crucifixion and res-urrection of Jesus Christ. Instead he was preaching the baptism of John and the coming kingdom of Christ. His message wasn't inaccurate, just incomplete. Priscilla and Aquilla didn't jump down his throat as soon as he walked away from the pulpit. Instead, "They invited him to their home and explained to him the way of God more adequately" (v. 26). That's a nice way of saying they witnessed to him. They took him in and filled in the blanks for him, probably over a home-cooked meal. They built a bridge and crossed it. They treated him with love, dignity, and respect as they gently told him the complete gospel message. ✳

Friendship-driven evangelists are relational in their evangelistic approach. They love others into the king-dom. Whereas a logic-driven evangelist's witnessing slogan could be "Let's start with a plan!" a friendship-driven evangelist's slogan could be "Let's start with a friend!" They tend to be listeners more than talkers. ✠

IMPROVE AS YOU PRACTICE

One of the biggest lessons that I have learned over the years of doing evangelism is that people change. When I first started doing evangelism I was much more direct, argumentative, and abrasive. Now I tend to be a better listener and much less prone to argue (although there are times). Some of these changes are due to spiritual maturity. Others are due to trial and error. Over the years you grow as a witness for Jesus Christ as you discover what is effective and what is not when it comes to evangelism. ✠

As you share your faith you become more and more skilled at it. If you are shy you become bolder. If you are a talker you learn how to listen. Your style becomes more and more balanced as you keep dependent on the Spirit of God. You become a reflection of Jesus Christ as He molds you and shapes you into His image. ✠

KEEP YOUR EYES ON THE ULTIMATE EVANGELIST

Jesus was the ultimate Evangelist. He is the best of each evangelistic style all wrapped up into one. He has all of their strengths and none of their weaknesses. ✠

He was the ultimate vision-driven evangelist. He told His followers to "make disciples of all nations" (Matthew 28:19). ✠

He was the ultimate action-driven evangelist. He went to the streets and boldly initiated conversations about the gospel message (Matthew 9:35). ❈

He was the ultimate logic-driven evangelist. He told His disciples to start first in Jerusalem and then go to Judea, Samaria, and, finally, to the ends of the earth (Acts 1:8). ❈

He was the ultimate friendship-driven evangelist. He felt the pains of others and listened to their stories as He skillfully turned the conversation toward the gospel (John 4). ❈

As we keep our eyes on Jesus, we will become more and more balanced in our approach. Over the years you will find God honing and sharpening and making you into a more effective witness. You will learn that there is a time to be relational and a time to be confrontational. You will learn that there is a time to see the big picture and a time to let logic drive the dialogue. You will discover that each style brings something different, unique, and powerful to the table. You will become like Jesus while being yourself . . . and that is the key to bringing it up and being yourself. ❈

So before you share your faith, make sure that you have all four tools in your survival kit sharpened and ready to go . . . the gospel, the radar, the funnel, and the test! ❈

Student Survival Tips

1. Thank God for your personal "witnessing wiring." Your style of sharing your faith is unique and is a special gift from God. Remember, you don't need to be like your pastor or youth pastor when sharing your faith. Be like you!

2. Remind yourself every morning to engage your witnessing radar. Ask God through His Holy Spirit to open your ears to hear how to turn everyday conversations with friends and strangers toward spiritual things and then "down the funnel."

3. Take the test!

Worst-Case Scenario

You are walking with a group of Christian friends on a downtown street. There you see a group of Christians who are yelling out things like "You people are going to burn in hell!" and "If you don't repent, God will condemn every one of you." The people who are in the area are either walking to the other side of the street to avoid these street preachers or yelling obscenities at them. The first thought in your mind is Well, that is just their style of evangelism. But then you think again. What do you do? ❊

THE TRIBAL CHALLENGE

Get together and practice role-playing, turning conversations about everyday things (movies, sports, relationships, school, news, etc.) into a conversation about Jesus. One person plays the lost person and the other the Christian, then switch! Remember to use each item in your survival kit and be as natural as possible. ❊

THE FINAL 5 CHAPTER

✷ "AND THEY LIVED HAPPILY EVER AFTER," THE CLASSIC STORYBOOK ENDING, IS BASICALLY HOW THE BIBLE ENDS. IN THE LAST CHAPTER OF REVELATION GOD TELLS US,

No longer will there be any curse. The throne of God and of the Lamb will be in the city, and his servants will serve him. They will see his face, and his name will be on their foreheads. There will be no more night. They will not need the light of a lamp or the light of the sun, for the Lord God will give them light. And they will reign for ever and ever. (Revelation 22:3–5)

After all the trauma and trouble of all of the plagues and famines and judgments and fire and brimstone of the book of Revelation, the very last chapter tells us how the story of humanity will end for those who are the children of God. It will end with us in perfect fellowship with the Lord minus sin, minus sadness, minus tragedy, minus death. We will be in absolute bliss as we worship the Lord and rule over this universe at His side forever and ever.

You see, future prophecy is really all about a love story!

From the Old Testament you can see this love story unfolding. The very first prophecy took place after Adam and Eve fell into sin. God prophesied this to the Satan-possessed snake of Genesis, "And I will put enmity between you and the woman, and between your offspring and hers; he will crush your head, and you will strike his heel" (Genesis 3:15).

The very first prophecy of the Bible is that, although mankind had blown it, God would send a Redeemer to crush the head of Satan and restore humanity to the heart of God.

All of the prophecies of the Old and New Testament directly or indirectly tie in to this love story. Even the prophecies concerning God's judgment were to serve as a warning so that those who heard them would repent and come back to the loving arms of their Creator. �

We need to communicate the gospel as the ultimate love story that just happens to be true! ✻

There is something about this generation of teenagers that just loves a good story. As a matter of fact, many teenagers don't judge reality by how logical it seems but by whether or not it emotionally affects them in some way. So when we communicate the gospel, we should share it as the ultimate love story that happens to be true. ✻

It is the most engaging and exciting story that could ever be told. It is full of twists and turns, romance and war, mystery and intrigue. It is the story of God's love affair with us! This love story unfolds over the course of human history and culminates with a wedding banquet . . . the marriage feast of the Lamb in Revelation 19:9. That is when we enter into an eternal marriage as the bride of Christ Himself! Talk about a love story. ✻

For this story came about after a battle that has erupted over the annals of history, a battle between God and Satan for the souls of mankind. This love story plays out in six powerful scenes that spell out the word "GOSPEL." ✻

od created us to be with Him.

ur sins separate us from God.

ins cannot be removed by good deeds.

aying the price for sin, Jesus died and rose again.

veryone who trusts in Him *alone* has eternal life.

ife that's eternal means we will be with Jesus forever.

THE SIX SCENES IN OUR STORY

SCENE #1
GOD CREATED US TO BE WITH HIM.

Once upon a time there lived a man named Adam and a woman named Eve. They lived in perfect bliss in a paradise. They were both beautiful people and had the closest relationship that you could imagine. Adam and Eve never argued. They never fought. They never complained. Sin wasn't an issue, because it wasn't around. ▓

They spent their time tending God's garden called Eden. Tending this garden was not as difficult as you would imagine. You see, there were no weeds. Tending was a matter of cultivating, pruning, and picking the fruit, which was big, beautiful, bountiful, and delicious. ✠

Adam and Eve didn't have to worry about wild animals. They were in perfect harmony with each other and with all of the animals, from the tortoise to the tiger, from the baboon to the bear. As a matter of fact, Adam had personally named all of the animals. It was no big deal to grab a lion by the mane and start wrestling around. You see, sin had not affected planet Earth yet, and only love was in the air. ✠

The first man and woman were in absolute love with each other and everything around them. They loved their existence, they loved their animal friends, and they loved each other. As a matter of fact, they were naked as the jaybirds that flew over their heads. This nakedness represented absolute transparency, honesty, authenticity, and innocence. Why? Because there was no sin and as a result no shame. There was nothing from which to hide. ✠

Not only was there absolute love and openness with each other and the creation around them, but with the Creator Himself. Adam and Eve were in a passionate love affair with each other as husband and wife. But there was one they loved even more . . . Jesus Christ, their Maker. With all of the animals God had said, "Let there be . . ." and there was. He spoke them into existence out of nothing. "Let there be fish in the sea" and *splash!* the ocean is full of all sorts of unique fish and teeming with life. "Let there be animals on the earth" and *bam!* all of a sudden the earth is packed with all sorts of unique birds and animals. With every other living thing, God created them with a word in rather broad categories. Cows, apes, hippopotamuses, and hyenas were all created at the same moment on one day with one sentence spoken from God. But He took special care to create man differently. ✴

On the sixth day of creation God looked all around Him and saw all of the beautiful trees, the wonderful animals, and amazing sea life and thought to Himself that all of this was good but still not complete. There was something missing. He wanted to form a special creation that was like Him in the sense that this creation would have mental, emotional, and spiritual dimensions. So He spoke to the other members of the Trinity and said, "Let us make man in our image, in our likeness, and let them rule over the fish of the sea and the birds of the air, over the livestock, over all the earth, and over all the creatures that move along the ground" (Genesis 1:26). ✴

The earth, and all of the animals on it, needed a ruler. Adam and Eve and the humanity that would spring from them were to be those "kings of the earth." So God made man, but not the way He created everything else. He didn't say, "Let there be man and woman." He took special care to form them uniquely and individually. ✴

God got His hands dirty . . . literally. On the sixth day of creation He found a big mud puddle and knelt down in it. Using the mud He sculpted the body of a man. Once the lifeless sculpture was complete, God leaned over the sculpted mud man and put His mouth on his nose and breathed into his nostrils "the breath of life." Immediately, this handcrafted mound of mud transformed into flesh and blood and bone. The mud became a man. ❊

Later, after noticing that all of the animals he named had a mate and he had none, Adam felt for the first time in his short creation that something was missing. He saw Mr. and Mrs. Rhino adoringly rubbing horns. He saw Mr. and Mrs. Orangutan lovingly picking bugs off of each other. And for the first time he felt a sense of loneliness. He was happy. But he was not complete. And he knew it. ❊

So God made Adam fall into a deep, deep sleep, and the first surgery was performed. Using His divine power He plunged His hand into the chest of Adam, pulled out a rib, and closed up the flesh. From that single rib God made Eve. When Adam woke from the deep sleep, God had a surprise for Adam. When he saw her beautiful naked body he exclaimed, "WHOOAAA-MAN!!!" And that became her title, "woman." ❊

Man and woman lived together in perfect harmony. They only had one rule that God had given them: Don't eat from the Tree of the Knowledge of Good and Evil. On the day you eat of it you will die. ❊

2 SCENE #2
OUR SINS SEPARATE US FROM GOD.

Everything was humming along quite nicely. Adam and Eve, the newlyweds, were starting their new lives together. They were busy cultivating the garden, learning about God's creation, and enjoying their married life.

Then one day Eve discovered something unique, something she had never seen before—a talking serpent.

This snake struck up a conversation with her and took her by complete surprise. Now remember, they had no fear of animals. Adam and Eve were designated by God as rulers over all creation. So she wasn't intimidated by this talking snake so much as she was intrigued by it.

Even Jeff Corwin or the Crocodile Hunter wouldn't know how to deal with this talking snake! This tricky serpent (who was controlled by Satan himself) asked Eve a question, "Did God really say, 'You must not eat from any tree in the garden'?" Eve responded quickly, "We may eat fruit from the trees in the garden, but God did say, 'You must not eat fruit from the tree that is in the middle of the garden, and you must not touch it, or you will die.'" So far so good. The snake tested Eve and she passed the test. She knew God's one rule for Adam and Eve.

So this Satan-possessed serpent tried a different approach. "You will not surely die. . . . For God knows that when you eat of it your eyes will be opened, and you will be like God, knowing good and evil" (Genesis 3:4–5).

Imagine the thoughts that must have rattled around in Eve's brain at that moment. *Being like God would be something good. Being able to discern good and evil would be an awesome power to have. And this snake says I won't die. Maybe God is holding something back from me. Maybe I will try just one bite of one piece of fruit and see what happens. Besides, it looks delicious. What harm could it do?*

With one bite the fate of humanity was sealed. Eve

took the bite and passed the piece of delicious fruit to her nearby husband. In that decisive moment of rebellion, Adam and Eve noticed something . . . they didn't drop dead. God had said that the day they ate of that fruit they would surely die. Maybe the serpent was right. But there were some immediate side effects. ❀

All of a sudden Adam and Eve felt something they had never experienced . . . shame. They sinned, and from that sin flowed guilt, and from that guilt flowed shame. They knew they were naked and were embarrassed by it. No longer were they open before God and each other. They had to cover their nakedness, so they wove together fig leaves into a coat of covering. ❀

Another side effect immediately kicked in . . . the fear of being in the presence of God in their sinful condition. God was coming to the Garden of Eden late in the afternoon for His regular time of fellowship with His two favorite creations. But instead of the normal welcoming, instead of the running to His presence, Adam and Eve hid. They hid in the trees and bushes of the garden wrapped in fig leaves because they were ashamed. ❀

God found them and confronted Adam. Adam blamed Eve. Eve blamed the serpent. The blame game began, and it hasn't stopped throughout all of human history. ❀

And there were some serious consequences for their direct violation of God's sole command to them. Work would no longer be a joy for Adam. Weeds would be his lot to pull. The weeds of the garden, the weeds of frustration, the weeds of impatience, and the weeds of confusion would pollute his life from that moment on. Childbirth would be a painful process for Eve. She would live a life of desire for her husband and frustration in their relationship. And the snake would be condemned to slither along the ground, being hated and hunted for all of its miserable life. ✜

But what must have confused Adam and Eve, what must have made them scratch their heads after the judgment was complete, was wondering this: *Didn't God say that we would die on the day we ate of the fruit?* ✜

What they didn't know at that moment, what they couldn't have known, was this—they did drop dead that day. They died spiritually. Their capacity for pleasing God was buried six feet under. From that moment on, their natural inclination would be to rebel against God. Their communion with God died that day, and the very essence of who they were meant to be spiritually became a lifeless corpse. And someday their bodies would catch up with their souls and they would be physically dead as well. ✜

From that defining moment in the garden, every child ever born (with the exception of Jesus) was born with a clenched fist of rebellion toward God. From the time of conception the infection begins—the infection of absolute rebellion toward God. Babies aren't born to die. They are born dead, spiritually. ✜

God rid Adam and Eve of the fig-leaf fashion and made the first sacrifice for their sin—an innocent animal. This animal died so that God could make two garments for Adam and Eve to wear, to cover their shame and hide their sinfulness from His holy eyes. ✜

Something about a blood sacrifice holds God's judgment back. Something in His nature demands payment and justice. If Adam and Eve were to survive, something or someone had to die in their place. ▓

Adam and Eve did eventually die. Hundreds of years later their bodies succumbed to the grave. Their souls died on the day they ate their fruit, and their bodies began to die that day. But the saddest thing was this: What died on the day of the "fruit incident" was their relationship with God. ▓

The first two scenes of our love story are depressing. But it gets worse before it gets better. ▓

3   SCENE #3
SINS CANNOT BE REMOVED BY GOOD DEEDS.

By now Adam and Eve had been booted out of the Garden of Eden and had accepted their lot of a damaged relationship with God. But life goes on, right? Well, kind of. Adam started working. And this work was nothing like the joyful mission that he had to accomplish at first. He got tired. He came home aching and complaining. In the meantime Eve got pregnant, and nine months later Cain was born. Later she gave birth to Abel. As the kids grew up, Mom and Dad were often breaking up the brotherly battles between these two polar opposite kids. Cain was a farmer. Abel was a shepherd. Cain was tough and rough. Abel was meek and mild. Cain was all about "getting ahead." Abel was all about pleasing God. ▓

TWO OFFERINGS

One day Cain and Abel brought their offerings to God. Cain brought some of his best fruits and vegetables to offer to God. Abel brought the firstborn lamb of the best of his flock and slaughtered it before God and offered it to Him. God loved Abel's offering and rejected Cain's. ✥

Why? It goes back to the Garden of Eden. God made the first sacrifice as an example to Adam and Eve (and for all of humanity to come) to show that the only thing that can cover the stain of sin is the blood of the innocent. Abel knew his God and made a sacrifice that would please Him. Cain didn't know his God and his offering was rejected. ✥

This moment of embarrassment infuriated Cain. His wimpy little brother's sacrifice was accepted by God, and his offering wasn't. Cain's offering came as a result of hard work, blood, sweat, and tears out in the fields, toiling under the hot sun. He worked harder for his offering than Abel did. He had the calluses to prove it. He labored night and day to produce that offering. It took months of effort. All Abel did was put a knife up to a lamb's throat and slice. This was an embarrassment that Cain was not going to forget or forgive. That anger boiled into an uncontrollable rage. ✥

One day he invited Abel out to the field and killed him. And so the world's first murder came from a religious feud between brothers. And it's been taking place ever since. ✥

THE CAINS VERSUS THE ABELS

Throughout history there have been those who have tried to please God with the fruit of their own labor. They offer their own good deeds and their commitment and their hard work as an offering to God. They work hard at religious acts of self-sacrifice, yet time and time again their offering is rejected by God. Meanwhile those believers in the Old Testament who knew that it wasn't about their hard work for God but the sacrifice of the innocent in their place for their sin simply put a knife to the throat of the innocent lamb or bull or goat and sliced.

Cain's offering has not stopped. It is seen in every religious institution or tribal ritual that seeks to be accepted by God as a result of self-effort. But God has been rejecting Cain's sacrifice since the beginning of time.

Even today Cain's offering is being made. Ask the typical person on the street, "What does it take to get to heaven?" Most likely the answer will revolve around doing some sort of good deeds. People think, *If I work hard enough and try hard enough and serve others enough, then God will let me into heaven and accept my "offering."* But those people are dead wrong . . . and it will lead to an eternal death in the flames of hell.

4 SCENE #4
PAYING THE PRICE FOR SIN, JESUS DIED AND ROSE AGAIN.

So let's sum up the story. God creates humanity to be in a love relationship with Him. They are living together in absolute harmony. But then the tempting mistress of sin ensnares humanity with the lustful lure of self-fulfillment. Humanity gives in and commits adultery against God Himself. No amount of human effort can bridge the gap between holy God and sinful mankind. An unending number of Cain-like sacrifices from men and women throughout the ages don't do the trick. The biggest breakup of human history has occurred, and death is the result. �

But this is when God takes the initiative. He chooses to take a drastic step to reunite with the ones He loves so much. He decides to send His own Son into the world to be the ultimate sacrifice. Infinitely more powerful than Abel's sacrifices or the countless animal sacrifices from the Israelites through many centuries, this sacrifice would result in the death of God's own Son. �

So two thousand years ago God sent His only Son, whom He loved with all of His heart, into the world. He formed Jesus in Mary's womb as the sinless God-man. The body of Jesus, unaffected by the ravages of sin, developed into a perfect little baby boy. He was unlike any of the other boys He grew up with in Nazareth. Yes, He was fully human. But He was completely God as well. Temper tantrums, rebellion, lust, and all the adolescent struggles were not temptations that Jesus gave in to. Why? Because He had no sinful nature. He had a human and divine nature that worked together in harmony for the glory of God. �

At the age of thirty His earthly ministry began. As a traveling evangelist, teacher, and miracle worker, He was busy ministering to the masses and pouring His life into His disciples. The sheer mass of people that began to follow Jesus forced Him to keep constantly on the move. These Israelites wanted Him to publicly proclaim Himself to be the deliverer of Israel and to establish

God's kingdom on earth. But Jesus had only one thing on His mind: Before He could establish a kingdom He must first redeem the ones He loved so much. He must first make the ultimate sacrifice. Three years after the start of His ministry He did.

It was a gruesome death. Beaten beyond recognition, whipped to the point of death, and nailed to a cross, the broken, bruised, and bloodied body of Jesus hung on that cross with the help of three nails and an indescribable love for you and me. Two of the phrases He screamed out while hanging on the cross changed the course of human history. The first phrase, "Eloi, Eloi, lama sabachthani?" means "My God, My God, why have You forsaken Me?" It was at that moment when God the Father took all of His anger that raged in His heart toward every sin that was ever committed or ever would be committed and He poured all of it on the body, spirit, and soul of Jesus. For the first time in all of eternity Jesus felt the sting of God's anger.

In that single moment Jesus absorbed all of the fury of God for all of the transgressions of man. Jesus took the hit for us . . . for all of us. He died so that we would not have to. He suffered so that we wouldn't need to. In that moment on the cross He felt the equivalent of all of the pain of all the flames of all the eternal torment that all the people who had ever lived or ever would live were headed for. It is almost as though God the Father squeezed all of the potential pain of everyone's eternity in hell into one huge bowl and poured it on the head of Jesus on that horrible and glorious day.

The second phrase that would change the course of humanity was "It is finished!" The price of sin had been paid in full. The ultimate sacrifice had been made once and for all. There was no longer a need for Abel's sacrifice. You see, Abel's sacrifice, and all of the animal sacrifices of the Old Testament, pointed to that one sacrifice . . . the one sacrifice that would not just cover over the shame of mankind but remove it for good. ▓

Remember that God made the first sacrifice to cover man's shame in Genesis chapter 3. But this sacrifice would do more than just remove the shame of sin. God made the first sacrifice. God the Son was the last sacrifice. His death removed not just the shame and the guilt and penalty, but the sin itself. ▓

Jesus died, and He rose from the dead three days later. He was seen by more than five hundred witnesses over the course of forty days. His resurrection proves that He was who He claimed to be. This was no mere man. He was much more than just a good teacher or miracle worker. He was God Himself . . . in the flesh. After forty days He ascended into heaven commanding His disciples to invade and persuade until He returns to be reunited with His bride, the love of His life . . . us. ▓

5 SCENE #5
EVERYONE WHO TRUSTS IN HIM *ALONE* HAS ETERNAL LIFE.

After the breakup, after the ultimate sacrifice, it gets personal. Jesus died for everyone. But if you were the only person on this earth, He would have died for you. As He hung upon the cross He had you in mind. And now He wants to get back together with us. ▩

So the question is, how? What do we have to do? The answer is simple . . . nothing. We do nothing. We don't try to make Cain's offering by trying to please God with all the religious or spiritual deeds we can come up with. We don't do anything. We just believe that what Christ has done on the cross is enough. We just trust in Him and Him alone to forgive us and welcome us back into His arms. ▩

The whole story of the New Testament is the story of Jesus with His disciples and through His disciples spreading this good news to everyone. The message they shared was simple . . . we don't have to stay at odds with God. Through our faith in His Son He will receive us back. We may stray from Him, but He will never stray from us! ▩

Now, please don't misunderstand this part of the story. It may sound too good to be true. It may sound too easy. But it is not. You see, we are more like Cain than Abel. We would rather try to earn it than to receive it simply by faith. We would rather trust in our own good deeds than to put our trust in Jesus and Him alone to make us acceptable to God. ▩

If we want to be reunited in a love relationship with God, it takes a trust in Him and Him alone. He won't accept us if we are trusting in anything else (good deeds) or anyone else (different gods) other than Him alone. ▩

But if we do trust Him alone, believing that He made the ultimate sacrifice for all of our sins, He accepts us without conditions. And once we enter into that relationship, it is permanent, which leads us to the final scene in our story.

6 SCENE #6
LIFE THAT'S ETERNAL MEANS WE WILL BE WITH JESUS FOREVER.

The final scene of this powerful play is in one sense the beginning of a new drama that will unfold over the course of eternity. All of those who have put their faith and trust in Jesus Christ alone for their deliverance will spend forever ruling and reigning with Christ.

Yes, the book of Revelation, as we said before, is full of the wrath of God toward rebellious humanity. But everything is building toward a wedding celebration. The culmination of thousands of years of broken hearts and dreams is when Jesus and humanity are wedded once and for all in the presence of the Father. That relationship that was shattered in the Garden is finally and fully restored. The love story will never again be short-circuited by sin, and it will never end.

What does this story mean for you? It means that when you trust in Jesus alone for the forgiveness of your sin, you enter into an unchangeable, unbreakable relationship with the lover of your soul. There will never be a divorce or even a separation. He loves you and will never leave you or forsake you. He won't let you leave either. He won't let slip away the relationship He worked so hard to restore.

So here is how the story ends: "Now the dwelling of God is with men, and he will live with them. They will be his people, and God himself will be with them and be their God. He will wipe every tear from their eyes. There will be no more death or mourning or crying or pain, for the old order of things has passed away" (Revelation 21:3–4).

The old order is over. The breakup is a distant memory. A new relationship between Jesus and His bride has begun. And it will never end.

And they lived happily ever after.

"THIS IS OUR STORY! THIS IS OUR CREED!"

These six scenes compile the story of Christianity. But these scenes also become points that we believe. In other words, the gospel is our story that we tell others, but it is also the creed that we believe ourselves.

A creed is a belief system in bullet form. That's how I want you to view the points of the GOSPEL acronym . . . as a creed to believe and a story to tell. In the next chapter we are going to use the six points of this creed and story to develop a very simple way of sharing your faith called the 2.6.2 Technique. This method is built around the GOSPEL story, so before you finish the Tribal Challenge it is my goal that you have mastered it completely.

Even when you tell the story in love, you will make a lot of people mad. Just like Cain got mad when God didn't accept the offering that he worked so hard to produce, people will often get angry when they understand that their offering doesn't matter. God's sacrifice is the only one that counts. 🔀

When you start telling others the good news that forgiveness of sins is a matter of simple faith and not hard work, the "You mean to tell me" people will show up. They will say things like,

"You mean to tell me that all a person has to do is trust in Jesus Christ and they are going to heaven?"

"You mean to tell me that all my good deeds don't count?"

"You mean to tell me that a mass murderer who trusts in Jesus Christ on his deathbed will go to heaven before a nice person who has never accepted Christ?"

"You mean to tell me that all I have to do is believe?" 🔀

That's one of the ways you know that you are sharing the gospel right. It was the same complaint Cain had. "You mean to tell me that I have been slaving under the hot sun to produce an acceptable offering to God, and it is rejected? You mean to tell me that Abel sacrifices a lamb, and just like that he is accepted by God?" The same kind of anger that flowed from Cain will flow from those who hate a message that seems too good to be true. 🔀

The gospel story is amazing, shocking, and scandalous. It is the ultimate love story that has to be shared with everybody who will listen . . . especially in these end times. ▓

In all of the talk about the coming of Jesus, don't freak out. Yes, there will be wars, famines, judgments, and such. But a happy ending is possible. As a matter of fact, if you trust in Jesus, a happy ending is guaranteed. I read the last chapter . . . we win. ▓

STUDENT SURVIVAL TIPS

1. Start a Bible reading program where you can read all of the story of the Bible in about one year. If you read three chapters a day, you can finish reading the whole Bible in one year! Take notes all along the way.

2. Memorize the GOSPEL acronym word for word. It will give you a basic outline to share the story of Christianity with your friends.

WORST-CASE SCENARIO

The body of Jesus is found buried in Jerusalem.
He didn't rise from the dead after all. What do
you do? (Hint: Read 1 Corinthians 15:12–32 to
see what Paul suggests we might as well do if
Jesus hadn't risen from the dead.)

P.S. His body won't be found. He has risen!
But what if?

THE TRIBAL CHALLENGE

Do a skit as a group that tells the story of all six
scenes of the story of Christianity. (Please stay
fully clothed for the Garden of Eden scene!)

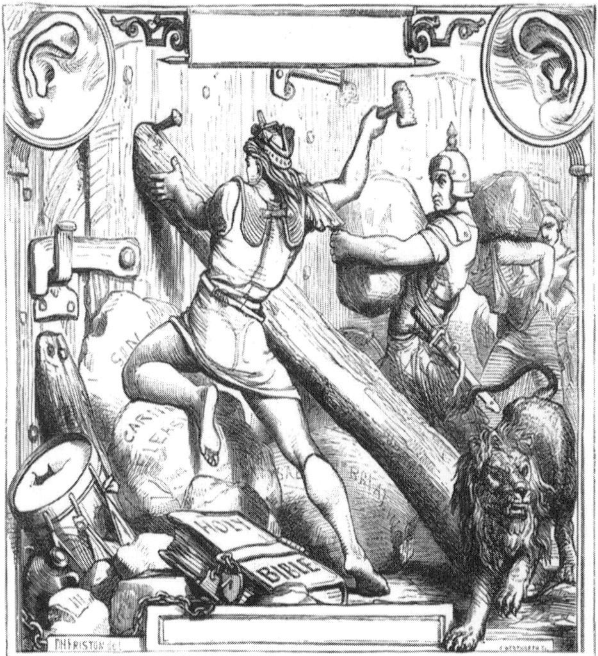

6

Fighting "666" with "262"

This calls for wisdom. If anyone has insight, let him calculate the number of the beast, for it is man's number. His number is 666″ (Revelation 13:18).

What is the number of the beast? Some believe that this 666 represents the unholy trinity—the Beast, the False Prophet, and the Antichrist. Others believe that it is merely some sort of marking system initiated by the Antichrist that somehow identifies those who are part of the "system." Those who get the mark can buy and sell. Those who don't will be hunted down and killed. ✠

Imagine a future newscast during the Tribulation time that goes something like this:

Today in the news there will be a special global news conference. While most experts don't know exactly what the press conference will reveal, one thing is sure: President Williams, the Global Alliance, and the religious community will give an unprecedented announcement that will dramatically affect the lives of every person on planet Earth. In recent months the Global Alliance has faced extensive criticism for its united efforts to identify and mark every person with a special encrypted microchip. This invisible code that acts as kind of a built-in ATM card also serves as a GPS Tracking System, all feeding into a centralized computer system. Although the vast majority of global citizens have received the mark, some who oppose these efforts argue that this is an invasion of privacy and an overthrowing of our rights. A fringe group of religious extremists believe that this marking is part of a global satanic conspiracy and is "the mark of the beast" mentioned in the biblical book of Revelation. But Global Alliance leaders argue that these efforts have nothing to do with spirituality and everything to do with practicality. They say that this is the only way to keep track of rogue criminals and terrorist groups. Recent efforts to criminalize the rejection of the mark have been met with some resistance, but experts believe that it is only a matter of time before extreme action is necessary. ✠

Whatever the actual mark will look like or accomplish, we know one thing for sure—it represents everything that God hates. It represents humanity in rebellion to God. It represents the "I can do it all by myself without God" attitude that pervades much of society today. It represents the spirit of the Antichrist that is alive and well today and has been for two thousand years. Listen to what the apostle John wrote: "Dear children, this is the last hour; and as you have heard that the antichrist is coming, even now many antichrists have come. This is how we know it is the last hour" (1 John 2:18). Later on he writes, "Every spirit that does not acknowledge Jesus is not from God. This is the spirit of the antichrist, which you have heard is coming and even now is already in the world" (1 John 4:3). ✠

What does all of this mean? It means ultimately that the spirit of Antichrist hates the gospel message. It means the mark of the Beast is at odds with the gospel of Jesus. ✠

So in this chapter you are going to learn how to fight the spirit of the Antichrist with the gospel truth. You are going to learn how to battle 666 with 262. ❇

WHAT IS THE 2.6.2 TECHNIQUE?

Quite simply, the 2.6.2 Technique is a method for sharing your faith. It is a pretty easy way to clearly share your faith. It's called the 2.6.2 because it has 2 opening questions, 6 simple points (the GOSPEL acronym that we went over in the last chapter), and 2 closing questions. ❇

I have used the 2.6.2 to train tens of thousands of teenagers across the nation to share their faith. What I really like about this method is that it gives someone a very simple starting point for communicating the gospel message. It shows you what to say. It explains how to bring it up, spell it out, and wrap it up. The more skilled you become at using it, the more naturally you will share your faith. ❇

But, bottom line, it is simply a method. It is the message of the gospel that transforms. Let's say that your best friend is on the opposite side of a river from you. And let's say that your friend is hurt and needs your help. The problem is that you need to get across this raging river so that you can help your friend. There are a lot of methods you could use to get across the river. You may look for a nearby bridge to run across. You may try to find a boat. You could even try to swim across the river. The point is to get across the river as quickly as possible. Methods are just a means to accomplish your mission. ✖

The same is true in sharing your faith. Your friend is hurting and in need of Christ on the other side of the river. There are a lot of ways you can get across. You can use "the bridge" or the 2.6.2 or three-story evangelism or an EvangeCube or a gospel tract. You could write a letter or invite him to a place where he is going to hear the gospel, like a Christian concert or a crusade. The point is this . . . it doesn't matter how you get across so much as it matters that you get across. Because the point is the gospel . . . not the method we use to cross the river of unbelief. ✖

As a matter of fact, I believe that the more skilled you become at sharing your faith using a method, the less you need the method. Once you've mastered the basics of the gospel message and a technique that communicates it, you can kind of pick and choose which particular method you want to use for that particular person. ✖

So look at the 2.6.2 as a starting point. It is easy to share. By the time you get done with this chapter and the survival tips, worst-case scenario, and tribal challenge at the end, you should be able to share your faith clearly and confidently with your friends. You will be able to cross the river. ✖

2 OPENING QUESTIONS

Why use questions? The answer is simple. Questions are a great way to get the attention of any audience and engage them in a dialogue about spiritual things. ✠

Nobody knew the power of asking key questions of a potentially interested audience more than Jesus Christ. Throughout His earthly ministry He asked key questions at precise times to seize the attention of His audience and drive His message home. Consider some of the many questions that Jesus asked others over the course of the three short years of His earthly ministry. ✠

"Who do you say I am?"
MATTHEW 16:15

"Why do you ask me about what is good?"
MATTHEW 19:17

"What do you think about the Christ?
Whose son is he?"
MATTHEW 22:42

"Why are you so afraid?"
MARK 4:40

"Do you still not understand?"
MARK 8:21

"What is written in the Law? . . . How do you read it?"
LUKE 10:26

"What is the kingdom of God like?"
LUKE 13:18

"John's baptism—was it from heaven, or from men?"
LUKE 20:4

"Do you believe this?"
JOHN 11:26

The list goes on and on. Jesus used questions to snag attention. We can too. Generally people love to talk about themselves. So let them. Actually, when you ask people questions, you are encouraging them to talk about themselves. What do they like? What do they dislike? What are they passionate about? What could they not care less about? What movies do they see, what books do they read, and what hobbies do they have? ✠

Perhaps James, the half brother of Jesus, gave us the greatest witnessing tip without even meaning to. In James 1:19 he writes, "My dear brothers, take note of this: Everyone should be quick to listen, slow to speak and slow to become angry." We need to learn to listen to others. Once people feel listened to *by* you, then they are much more likely to listen *to* you. ✠

OK. Let's pretend that you are in a conversation with your friend, classmate, teammate, or relative who doesn't know Christ. You are asking questions and you are getting answers. What do you do next in your plan to proclaim? ✠

LOOK FOR FORKS IN THE ROAD
....

Picture a conversation as a journey down an old country road. Things are just truckin' right along when all of a sudden you have a quick decision to make. Right before you is a fork in the road. If you stay on the current path, you will end up with your standard trite and polite conversation. But if you take the turn, you will end up across the border in the land of spiritual subjects. ✠

You have to constantly be on the lookout for these natural forks in the road. Every conversation becomes a potential opportunity to talk to someone about spiritual things. This is when your witnessing radar must be fully engaged. Using questions steers the conversation toward the funnel and then down the spout. ✠

THE STORY OF ANNA
....

Anna was a waitress at a restaurant that I used to go to just about every day to study. One day she looked especially sad. I asked her how she was doing. She said not well. I asked her why. She explained to me that her daughter was into all the wrong things and that she was getting stuck with the bill. I continued to ask questions, and she continued to open up. Finally, she told me that she had been seriously contemplating suicide.

"Why would God allow me to go through the things that I am going through, Greg?" she asked in utter frustration. Boom! There was the fork in the road.

"Well, Anna, I don't know. But I do know this. God

went through a whole lot more for us than we have ever gone through."

"What do you mean, Greg?"

"Well, Anna, two thousand years ago God lost His Son. . . ."

Over the next few moments I was able to lay out the gospel to Anna right there in the restaurant as she listened intently. I took the fork in the road. In the next few minutes we had a powerful talk about the plan of salvation. Since then we have talked several more times about the message of Christ. Now she is usually the one to bring it up! �֍

LEARN WHICH QUESTIONS
YOU CAN USE

Actually, when you get good at this, you will be able to make up your own questions on the spot. But that takes a lot of time and prayer and practice. It takes having your witnessing radar and your brain fully engaged. It also takes a deep dependence on the Spirit of God to give you wisdom on what questions to ask. �֍

In the meantime I will give you a list of pre-set questions you can use to turn a conversation toward the funnel of "spirituality" and down through the spout of Jesus as "the way." ✖

QUESTIONS TO PICK FROM:

1. What are your spiritual beliefs?
   (God? Heaven? Hell? Etc.)
2. Would you mind if I share with you what I believe?

1. Do you know for sure that you are going to heaven
   when you die?
2. If I could tell you how you can know for sure, would
   that be good news?

1. How did the terrorist attacks of 9-11 change your
   view of life and death?
2. May I tell you why I am not afraid to die?

1. What are your religious beliefs?
2. Do you want to know why I believe in a relationship
   with God and not a religion?

1. Do you go to church anywhere?
2. What does your church teach that a person has to do
   to get to heaven?

   *If the person doesn't go to church anywhere, ask,
   "Did you know that our church teaches that you
   don't have to go to church or even be good to get to
   heaven?"*

1. Who do you think Jesus was?

2. Did you know that the Bible teaches that He was fully God and fully man and He came to save the world?

Pick which questions fit your witnessing wiring the best (vision-driven, action-driven, logic-driven, or friendship-driven) or make up your own. Remember, the more you have your witnessing radar engaged, the more you pray and practice, the better you will get at steering the conversation toward spiritual things without pre-set questions. In the meantime, pick which questions fit your personality the most and memorize them word for word. �֎

Remember that the best and most natural opportunities to share the gospel take place in the natural ebb and flow of everyday conversation. But turning conversations toward the gospel doesn't happen automatically. It takes practice, wisdom, and time to get skilled at naturally turning conversations toward Christ. So have your radar on all of the time and seize the opportunities when they naturally arise. In the meantime, memorize two of the above questions that fit you the best so that if the conversation doesn't naturally arise you can "get the party started." ✖

This is probably a pretty good time to say something about bringing up the conversation of the gospel. Some Christians say that if you can't bring it up naturally after building a relationship over a long period of time, then you shouldn't bring it up "abruptly" at all. I fully agree that we as believers should be building relationships with those who don't know Christ and seek to naturally bring it up at the right time. We don't want to be "bullhorn" Christians who "cram and ram" the gospel down the throats of those who don't know Jesus. But there is something else I want you to think about when sharing the gospel: People's eternal souls are at stake. If they don't hear the gospel and believe, they will die and go to hell someday. So be loving, kind, and wise . . . but bring it up.

6 POINTS

In chapter 5 we went over these points in detail. So in this chapter I am going to give you two simple ways to communicate these six points. One way is verbally and the other is visually.

VERBALLY

This is when you basically share the story of the gospel using the GOSPEL acronym as a guide. The GOSPEL acronym becomes a mental outline that helps you remember each key scene in this awesome story.

So maybe the conversation goes something like this:

> "So here is the story. **God created us to be with Him.** He made all of humanity to be in perfect harmony with Him, but then mankind disobeyed Him, and as a result **our sin separated us from God.** You see, God is a holy God. He hates sin and

can't be around it. And those **sins cannot be removed by our good deeds.** That's what most people think . . . that if you are religious enough or nice enough God will let you into heaven someday. But no number of good deeds will ever get rid of our sins. So two thousand years ago God sent His Son Jesus into the world. He lived a perfect life because He was fully God and fully human. And then, **paying the price for our sin, Jesus died and rose again.** He died in our place for our sins. And now He says that **everyone who trusts in Him alone has eternal life.** That's it—if you trust in Him and Him alone you receive the free gift of eternal life, and **life that's eternal means that we will be with Jesus forever.**"

Now this is a really basic conversation. Usually there is give-and-take, questions and answers. But the beauty of the six points is that they give you a mental outline that helps you remember where you were when there are those natural breaks in the conversation. ⌘

A lot of times the conversation goes down many paths. But no matter how many paths it may take, you can always weave it back to this story (and creed). ⌘

VISUALLY

I love this illustration. It helps you communicate the gospel visually. It is basically using some hand motions and an object (rock, wallet, pen, paper, can, whatever) to visually illustrate the 6 points. Here it goes:

❊ Pretend this hand is humanity and this hand is God. *God created us to be with Him. (Then grasp your hands together.)*

❊ But then *our sins separated us from God* (use a book, wallet, water bottle or something else to represent sin), because although God loves us, He hates sin.

❊ And our *sins could never be removed by good deeds,* so there is no way that just trying to be a good person could get us reunited with God.

4

So, Jesus (hold up the hand representing God) came to the earth 2000 years ago, became a man, and lived a perfect life. Then *paying the price for sin, Jesus died and rose again.* (Have the "Jesus" hand take the sin off of us, drop the object to the ground, and hold up the Jesus hand.)

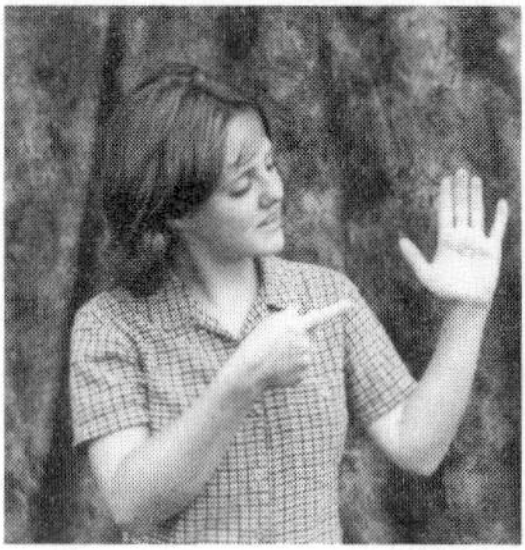

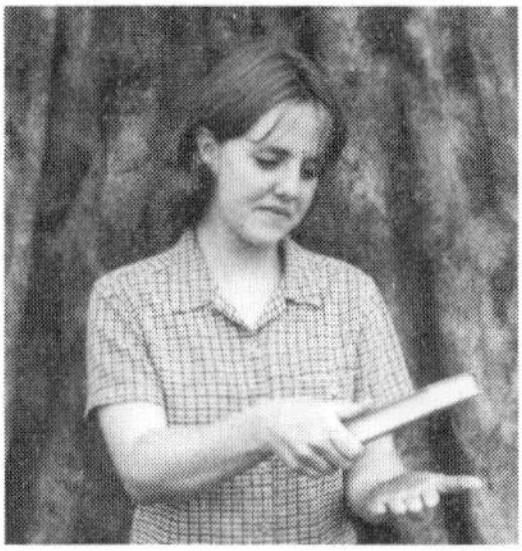

5

Now, *everyone who trusts in Him alone has eternal life.* (Point to the "Jesus" hand.)

6

And *life that's eternal means we will be with Jesus forever in heaven.* (Clasp hands together.)

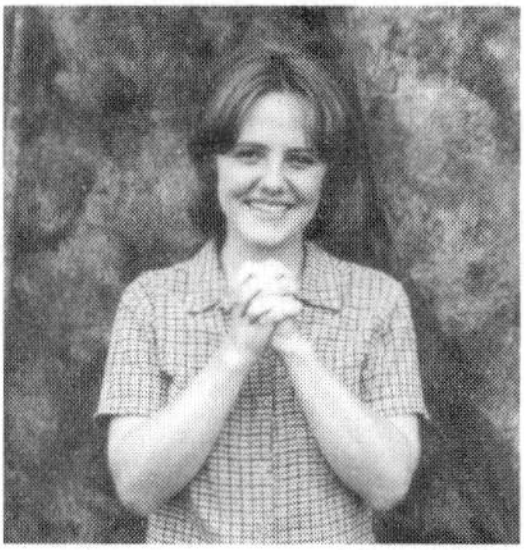

2.6.2
POINTS

Here are some optional illustrations that you can weave into your presentation of the gospel. What works especially well is if you can find illustrations from your own life. But here are a few great illustrations to get you started.

THE BURNT CAKE
(to illustrate why good deeds don't work)

Let's say that I baked you a cake and burned it badly. If I were to cover it in white frosting and give it to you, the cake would still be burnt even though you couldn't see it. As soon as you bit into it you would know. Putting white frosting on a burnt cake doesn't change the fact that the cake is ruined. Covering our sinful lives with good deeds doesn't change the fact that we have sinned. God sees right through the "frosting." 🏵

THE OCEAN
(to illustrate why we all fall short of God's requirements)

Imagine that you and I are standing on the coast of California and we decide to swim to Hawaii. Maybe you make it fifteen miles and I make it five or so. It doesn't matter. Because both of us are going to end up on the bottom of the ocean. Why? It is too far for anyone to swim. It is humanly impossible. In the same way, if we try to make it to heaven by living a good life, then we are going to fall way short. Why? According to the Bible we have to be as good as God to get into heaven. Nobody is. So we all miss the mark of God's impossible standard. And God won't give a few points to one person because he or she is "pretty good" and some other person is "really bad."

THE TRUCK
(to illustrate Jesus dying in our place)

Let's say that you are walking across a busy street and not paying much attention. All of a sudden a big, speeding truck comes out of nowhere and is headed straight at you. But you don't see it coming. Somebody standing on the street corner sees what is about to take place and with blazing speed runs into the middle of the street and pushes you out of the way right at the last minute. The speeding truck hits the other person instead. He absorbs the full impact of the truck. He dies in your place. The person sacrificed his life for you. In the same way, the anger of God was headed straight at us because of our sins. Jesus pushed us out of the way and absorbed the full impact of God's anger for our sin. He died in our place. He sacrificed His life for ours.

YOUR STORY

As you are telling the story of the gospel you may feel compelled to share your own personal testimony. In other words, you may want to tell the person the story of how you became a Christian. In Acts 26 Paul told his personal testimony to King Agrippa. He basically used a simple formula to share his testimony. We can use that same little formula that revolves around three simple points (before, during, after). ✷

BEFORE

✷ What life was like for me before I became a Christian

✷ How I felt inside

✷ What my relationships were like

✷ What I used to believe about God

DURING

✷ How I heard the gospel message

✷ What I thought of it at first

✷ When I finally accepted it

AFTER

✷ What life has been like for me since I became a Christian (struggles and all)

✷ How I feel inside

✷ The ways it has changed my relationships

✷ How it has affected every aspect of my life

USING SCRIPTURE
....

I want to really encourage you to use Scripture as much as possible. That doesn't mean that you have to carry a Bible around with you all of the time, but it does mean that you put at least a few salvation verses to memory.

Even if those you are witnessing to don't believe that the Bible is God's Word, that doesn't erase the power of God's Word. Listen to what God tells us in Isaiah 55:11: "So is my word that goes out from my mouth: It will not return to me empty, but will accomplish what I desire and achieve the purpose for which I sent it."

Basically this verse is saying that God sends His Word on a mission that will be accomplished. So when we share God's Word with others, it will do something in their souls, whether they believe it or not.

Another place the Bible says this,

or the word of God is living and active. Sharper than any double-edged sword, it penetrates even to dividing soul and spirit, joints and marrow; it judges the thoughts and attitudes of the heart. Nothing in all creation is hidden from God's sight. Everything is uncovered and laid bare before the eyes of him to whom we must give account. (Hebrews 4:12–13)

These verses paint the picture of God's Word as a sharp sword that opens up the souls of those we are talking to and lays bare their deepest secrets and thoughts.

It convicts and convinces. Even if somebody doesn't believe in the sword of the Lord, keep wielding it. The slice of cutting-edge truth may convince them yet.

Here are a few verses to get started with:

G

God created us to be with Him.

GENESIS 1:26

O

Our sins separate us from God.

GENESIS 6:5–6

S

Sins cannot be removed by our good deeds.

TITUS 3:5

P

Paying the price for sin, Jesus died and rose again.

1 CORINTHIANS 15:3–4

E

Everyone who trusts in Him alone has eternal life.

JOHN 6:47

L

*Life that's eternal means we will
be with Jesus forever.*

REVELATION 22:5

2 CLOSING QUESTIONS

"DOES THAT MAKE SENSE?"

It is vital to make sure people get it. This question helps you know if they understand. ✖

If they say no, you can simply review what you have already shared with them. You can try rephrasing things a little bit to be even clearer. You can ask the same "Does that make sense?" question after each point of the G-O-S-P-E-L message. You can ask them which part they are having a hard time understanding.✖

If they say yes to the "Does that make sense?" question, you can move on to the final question:

"WOULD YOU TRUST IN JESUS RIGHT NOW AS YOUR ONLY HOPE OF GOING TO HEAVEN?"

This is the key question. This is when you are asking the person to make a decision. Will the person receive or reject Jesus Christ as his or her only hope of going to heaven? That word *only* is the focal word. Jesus is not *a* way to heaven; He is *the* way to heaven. Jesus put it this way in John 14:6, "I am the way and the truth and the life. No one comes to the Father except through me." ✖

Pretty blunt statement, huh? Jesus is the only way to hope and heaven. A lot of people go into the funnel but refuse to go through the spout. But there is no other stairway to heaven but Jesus Christ. When you ask people to believe in Jesus Christ, you are essentially asking them to forsake every other way, every other avenue to heaven. ✖

Several years ago I went to India to preach a series of crusades. In eighteen days I preached fifty-six times to a total of about thirty thousand people. Most of these "crusades" took place at Catholic schools where I was invited to preach to the mostly Hindu children who attended these private institutions. ✠

Hindus have many gods. As I preached I had to continually focus on the fact that Jesus is not *a* way to heaven but *the* way to heaven. To illustrate this, after I presented the gospel to the children I would bring a chair onto the stage. I would put one foot up on the chair and keep one foot on the floor. I would then ask the children if I were placing my full trust in that chair. They would scream back "No!!!!" "What do I need to do if I am going to fully trust in the chair?" I would ask. "Stand on the chair!" they would yell back. For some reason when I would stand on the chair they would yell and applaud and laugh in approval. I would then ask, "Now am I fully trusting in the chair?" "Yes!!!" they would howl. "In the same way, children, if you want to go to heaven you must place your full trust in Jesus. You cannot trust in Jesus and some other god to take you to heaven. You must believe in Jesus and Jesus alone, turning your back on every other god and trusting in Jesus alone as your only hope of going to heaven." ✠

I would finish the invitation standing on the chair, encouraging the children to stand on Jesus alone. They got it. Thousands of Hindu children came to Christ in those eighteen days. It was a powerful event to witness. ✠

American teenagers today are much more Hindu than Christian. As you share the gospel with friends, just remember that they may believe that Jesus is God. But they may also believe that as long as Buddhists, or Mormons, or Muslims are sincere in their faith they will make it to heaven. ❖

That's why the word *only* is so important in the final question. It must be emphasized that Jesus is the only way. If a person doesn't accept this, then he or she doesn't really accept Christ. ❖

What if people say no to the final question? Simply ask them "Why?" They may have reasons that they don't want to believe it. Address their issues the best that you can. But remember you can never talk someone into the kingdom. The Spirit of God must awaken the mind and quicken the soul. Try your best and trust your God. ❖

SHORT JUMP/LONG JOURNEY

For some teenagers you talk to, it will be a short journey to the Cross. You will go through the 2.6.2 and they will be ready. God has been preparing their hearts, and as soon as you share the gospel with them they will accept Christ. When that happens, it is an awesome experience. But often it takes a lot longer. That's where the long journey comes in. ❖

When I was a child in inner-city Denver, I was in awe of my uncles. Three of them had won titles as body builders. One of them was a Golden Gloves boxer. All of them were tough as nails. But one by one they encountered someone even tougher. His name was Jesus Christ. 🏵

I remember when rugged Uncle Jack, rippling with muscles, covered in tattoos, and drenched with attitude, came to Christ. The encounter completely turned the direction of his life. He was transformed from a street fighter to a street preacher in nothing flat. 🏵

Uncle Bob was a bouncer in a downtown bar who surrendered his soul to Christ after a brawl that left his victim without a heartbeat. In the back of a squad car as the paramedics sought to resuscitate the dying man, Uncle Bob called out to God, "If they bring him back, God, I will serve You with all of my heart." They did . . . and he did. One year later he was in Bible college. To this day he and his family are faithful witnesses for Jesus Christ. 🏵

Things weren't quite as simple with my uncle Richard. He was that one uncle who wasn't at all open to the gospel message. 🏵

I never really knew Uncle Richard well growing up. I just knew that he had moved to Phoenix, Arizona, as a young man to make his fortune in business. And that's exactly what he did. 🏵

He, like my other uncles, was tough as nails. I had heard the stories of the fights that he had been in grow-ing up. My family told me about the time that he jumped through the passenger window of a moving car full of six guys who were out to get him and his brothers. He took all of them on as the car wove back and forth down the road for two or three blocks. 🏵

I had talked to Uncle Richard only a few times growing up. The only times I can remember were a couple brief conversations on the phone. ▓

After most of my uncles had come to Christ, they began to pray for Richard to become a Christian as well. But when they brought it up, he would stop them cold in their tracks. He didn't want to talk about it. ▓

Then Grandpa died of a sudden, massive heart attack. Uncle Richard flew up from Phoenix to be with all of us at the funeral. I was fifteen years old at the time. ▓

I had the opportunity to give the gospel at my grandpa's funeral. Hundreds had crammed into the small mortuary as the funeral service began. My mind was reeling and my heart was racing. This was the biggest crowd I had ever spoken in front of. I knew that there were people in the audience that needed to hear the gospel. But there was one person especially on my mind—Uncle Richard. I knew that he didn't know Christ. ▓

The best that I knew how I gave the gospel and gave an invitation for people to respond. Many did. But Uncle Richard didn't. My family was crushed because of the dual loss—the loss of Grandpa and the loss of Richard's soul. ▓

Soon after the funeral I wrote a letter to Uncle Richard that expressed to him how much I hoped and prayed that he would become a Christian. He never responded to my letter. Not a phone call. Not a postcard. Nothing. ▓

Almost twelve years later Richard was coming into town again for another funeral . . . his own. He had melanoma. This deadly cancer had spread throughout his whole body. He flew back to have one last family reunion and say good-bye to those he loved.

But we wanted to see him again. We wanted to see him in heaven. Still, he made it clear that he didn't want to talk about it. Uncle Bob gave him a letter that told him how much he meant to him and that he wanted to see him in heaven someday. Richard cried when he read the letter but still didn't want to talk about death, or heaven, or "religion," or anything of a spiritual nature. Finally my uncle Bob talked him into coming to Grace Church (where I was the preaching pastor at the time) the next day with the rest of the family. He was hesitant at first but finally agreed.

I'll never forget the sight. My uncles, aunts, and cousins, crammed into the two last pews. These huge muscle-bound believers had only one thing on their minds . . . Richard's salvation. They prayed the whole service because they knew that at the end of my sermon I would give the gospel.

After painstakingly laying out the message of salvation, I had everybody bow their heads and close their eyes. I then asked for those who had trusted in Christ as their Savior that day to raise their hands. It was something to see. Without a moment's hesitation Richard and his wife Tarin thrust their hands into the air. I could hear the sobs of my family (they had been peeking). When they saw Richard and Tarin raise their hands, they just began to cry.

In the airport later that day, Richard pulled Bob aside, put his arm around him, and said, "Guess what happened, brother. I am going to be in heaven." Bob wrapped his arms around Richard's frail, cancer-emaciated frame and wept. They said good-bye for the last time, knowing that the next time they would see each other would be in glory.

Richard called later and asked me to give the gospel at his memorial service in Arizona. He had been witnessing to his family and friends, and he thought that if I gave the gospel at his memorial then more would have the opportunity to trust in Christ. The last days of his life he was concerned about the lost souls of those around him. He wanted others to hear the good news of salvation through Jesus Christ.

On August 24, 1995, Richard Mathias met his Savior. After more than fifty years of life on earth, Richard finally breathed his last. The next time he opened his eyes he was in heaven . . . after a long, long journey.

Maybe you have some friends or family members like my uncle Richard. Keep praying. Keep sharing. For some it's a short jump; for others it's a long journey.

Student Survival Tips

1. Pick the questions that fit you the best.

2. Memorize the 2.6.2 Technique.

3. Practice until you have it down word for word.

4. Personalize it and make it your own (opening questions, illustrations, your testimony, etc.).

WORST-CASE SCENARIO

You have some friends at school that you think
are all Christians. You have prayed together at
lunch and have had a lot of conversations
about the Lord. One day as you are talking to
them you see that one of them has a Book of
Mormon. You ask what he is doing with that
and he tells you that all of them are Mormons.
You had no idea. They begin to tell you
Mormonism is really Christian and the
Mormon church is misunderstood. What do
you say? ▩

THE TRIBAL CHALLENGE

Memorize the 2.6.2 and spend thirty minutes
role-playing sharing the gospel with each
other. Try to be as natural as possible as you
share the gospel, and remember the funnel,
the radar, and the test! ▩

WORST-CASE WITNESSING SCENARIOS

7

⌗ JUST THINK OF SOME OF THE WORST-CASE SCENARIOS THAT ARE GOING TO BE AROUND DUR-ING THE TIME OF TRIBULATION ON THE EARTH. IMAGINE BEING A CHRISTIAN DURING THOSE SEVEN YEARS OF ABSOLUTE JUDGMENT ON THE

EARTH! BEING CHASED AROUND BY THE ANTICHRIST AND HIS TROOPS, HIDING FROM ANTI-CHRISTIAN ZEALOTS WHO WILL FLOOD THE EARTH, AND ENDURING ALL OF THE FAMINES, PLAGUES, EARTHQUAKES, AND CATASTROPHES OF THE BOOK OF REVELATION. TALK ABOUT WORST-CASE SCENARIOS. WHATEVER ONES YOU ARE FACING RIGHT NOW ARE NOTHING COMPARED TO WHAT CHRISTIANS WILL ENDURE DURING THE TRIBULATION! ✖

That is then. This is now. ✖

But let's face it. We all have our own worst-case scenarios that we endure in life, in relationships, and, sometimes, in witnessing. ✖

This chapter is all about troubleshooting those worst-case witnessing scenarios so that we know what to do when we face them. And believe me, if you start sharing your faith and living your faith as though you actually mean, it there will be trouble . . . lots of it. ✖

In this chapter I want to prepare you to face five worst-case scenarios that you may encounter while sharing your faith so that you know what to do. I have faced each of these scenarios myself and have learned through trial and error how to face them effectively. At the end of this chapter you and your tribe are going to make up your own worst-case witnessing scenarios, so have your brain fully engaged throughout the following pages. ✖

WORST-CASE
WITNESSING SCENARIO #1
YOU ARE WITNESSING TO A
PERSON WHO WANTS TO ARGUE,
AND YOU HAVE NO IDEA HOW
TO RESPOND.

So there you are sharing your faith with someone, and all of a sudden the person begins to ask you questions like, "How do you know there is a God?" and "Isn't the Bible full of mistakes?" You can feel your heart pounding in your chest and the adrenaline rushes throughout your body as the discussion accelerates into a debate. Pretty soon this person is saying things like, "Christians are all alike . . . hypocrites" and "You don't really believe all of this stuff, do you?" In those moments when your heart is beating fast, your mind is racing even faster, your blood pressure is through the roof, and your mouth is about to launch a counterattack, in those moments you have a choice to make.

The first and most obvious choice that you can make is to engage into a full-out, no-holds-barred cage match of argumentation. You can yell right back and accuse and be just as mean-spirited and angry.

The problem with this response is obvious. It's hard to convince somebody of the love of Christ with a pointing finger, a clenched fist, and a raised voice. Yes, you may win the argument, but if you lose the soul, then who cares? ✂

Let me be completely honest here . . . there have been times I have blown it in this area. When I was a teenager sharing my faith, there were times that a person got in my face and I got right back in his face. These toe-to-toe verbal exchanges almost never ended with the person putting his faith and trust in Christ. So let's rule out option #1 when it comes to dealing with this worst-case witnessing scenario. ✂

The second option is to back off completely and not discuss the person's questions at all. In this option you could say, "Well, I don't want to debate. You have your beliefs and that's fine. I don't want to cram my Christianity down your throat." ✂

The problem with this option is that it robs you of the chance of reaching that person for Jesus Christ. It tells the person that it's OK to believe what he believes, when in all reality it is not. Your friends could end up in hell if you use this strategy. ✂

The final and, in my opinion, best option is to engage but not enrage. This means that you must learn the fine skill of defending your faith without being offensive. Here are some hints to help you do this:

REFUSE TO ARGUE. CHOOSE TO DISCUSS.

Paul the apostle, who had some pretty intense discussions about Christianity throughout his career, wrote these powerful words:

nd the Lord's servant must not quarrel; instead, he must be kind to everyone, able to teach, not resentful. Those who oppose him he must gently instruct, in the hope that God will grant them repentance leading them to a knowledge of the truth, and that they will come to their senses and escape from the trap of the devil, who has taken them captive to do his will. (2 Timothy 2:24–26)

Notice the phrases he uses: "must not quarrel," "kind to everyone," "not resentful," and "gently instruct." That means that we must be loving as we are confronting people's belief systems. Why? Paul gives this powerful answer, "That they will come to their senses and escape from the trap of the devil." Paul reminds us that "they" are not the enemy. They are victims of the devil. When we engage them in a discussion about Christianity, we are doing it with the purpose of rescuing them from the clutches of the Evil One. ✠

USE THE "4-1 DEFENSIVE FORMATION"

One of the teen evangelism training conferences that we do at Dare 2 Share is themed "Game Day." This theme uses sports as an analogy for sharing your faith. The 2.6.2 is your offensive play, and the 4-1 defensive formation is how you defend your faith. This simple formation revolves around four questions and one statement. ✠

THE FOUR QUESTIONS

These questions, developed by my good friends Bill Jack and Andrew Heister, are excellent when it comes to lovingly nudging people to the "end" of their belief system. As we learned in the last chapter, Jesus was a master at using questions as a tool to pry open the minds of His listeners. As Bill Jack told me, "You can either use these questions as a sledgehammer or a pry bar. If you use them as a sledgehammer, you will destroy their arguments and the person as well. If you use them as a pry bar, you will pry open the mind of the person you are talking to so that he can think outside of the box of his preconceived notions."

Let's take a look at each of these questions:

1 QUESTION #1
WHAT DO YOU MEAN BY THAT?

This is a question of clarification. For instance, maybe a conversation goes something like this:

> "Hey, I'm already a Christian," your friend says.
>
> "What do you mean by 'Christian'?" you ask.
>
> "Well, I was born in America," she responds.
>
> "Being born in America doesn't make you a Christian. Being born in a garage doesn't make you a car."

This question of clarification helps both of you understand what you mean by certain phrases or words. It helps you get what people mean by what they are saying.

QUESTION #2
HOW DO YOU KNOW THAT TO BE TRUE?

This question pushes just a little bit. You are asking people for some evidence to what they believe. But be ready for them to push back just a little as well. They may ask you the same question. One of these conversations may go something like this:

"There is no God."

"How do you know that to be true?"

"I just know it."

"So you have been everywhere in the universe?"

"Well, no."

"And you know everything."

"Well, no."

"Then, how can you know there is no God? Would you at least admit that there is a possibility that there is a God?"

QUESTION #3
WHAT DIFFERENCE HAS IT MADE IN YOUR LIFE?

This is a question that pushes people to think about whether or not their belief system gives them purpose and meaning. For instance, if someone is an atheist and doesn't believe in God, then his meaning and purpose is defined only by the here and now. This question gets people to think about a broader, more universal purpose that extends beyond their lives on this earth. This meaning and purpose is found ultimately in the message and person of Jesus Christ.

4 QUESTION #4
WHAT IF YOU ARE WRONG?

I was on my way to Fort Wayne, Indiana, with the rest of the Dare 2 Share team to do a training conference on evangelism for hundreds of high school students when I met Lyn. She was in the seat next to me on the cramped commuter flight between Chicago and Fort Wayne.

She asked me why we were all headed to Indiana. I told her about the conference. As soon as I mentioned it was a "Christian" conference, she begin to hammer me with question after question. "Do you believe that Jesus is the only way to heaven?" "What about the Jews, Hindus, and Muslims?" "What happens to those who reject Jesus?" were just a few of the questions that Lyn asked me. To be honest, I wasn't much in the mood. I had a lot of computer work to do and was busy jamming away on my laptop. But God's Spirit had obviously opened a door of opportunity. So I took it. I responded with the classic apologetic arguments of C. S. Lewis and Josh McDowell. I explained to her that Jesus is either Lord, a lunatic, or a liar because He claimed again and again to be God in the flesh. From the hundreds of prophecies about Jesus that were completely fulfilled to the weight of eyewitness testimony, I stacked the evidence of Christ's deity before her. She didn't blink.

"I believe that as long as you are sincere you will be OK," she retorted. 🏵

"What about Hitler? He was sincere," I said. Again, she was cemented firmly in her convictions that my conclusions were too "narrow-minded." After several minutes of loaded discussion I realized that I was getting nowhere. So I asked her one of the four questions, "Lyn, let me ask you one thing. What if you are wrong?" 🏵

"What do you mean?" she asked hesitantly. 🏵

"What if you are wrong? What if there is a real heaven, a real hell, and a real Jesus whom you are rejecting as your Savior? What if when you die you stand before His throne and have to give an account of why you didn't believe? What if all your conclusions about who goes to heaven are wrong and what the Bible says is right?" 🏵

Her mouth dropped wide open. Up until then she had a comeback for every shred of evidence I laid before her. This time she had none. I must commend her for her honesty. She looked in my eyes and said, "What if I am wrong? I have never even thought about that possibility! What a good question! I am going to have to ask my husband about that when I get off the plane. What if we are wrong?" 🏵

The last time I saw Lyn was at the baggage claim area in Fort Wayne asking her husband, "Honey, what if we are wrong about all this stuff that we believe?" Seeds of doubt were sown in the hopes that the seeds of faith would sprout. 🏵

These questions work. They make honest people think about the true reliability of their own belief systems. Use them, but not as a construction worker uses a jackhammer, with aggressiveness and abandon. Use these key questions as a skillful surgeon uses a scalpel, with precision, wisdom, and care.

THE ONE STATEMENT

OK, so you are using the four questions and they are using them on you and then *BAM*! they ask you a question that you don't have the answer to. What do you do? You use the one statement, "I don't know, but I'll find out." You find an answer and get it back to them. This is the argument buster that we went over in chapter 3 on Fear Factors.

2

WORST-CASE WITNESSING SCENARIO #2

YOU LEAD SOMEBODY TO CHRIST AND HAVE NO IDEA HOW TO HELP THE PERSON GROW IN HIS BRAND-NEW FAITH.

OK, this is the best of the worst-case scenarios . . . at the very least the person is going to heaven. But we don't want to just get people into heaven someday; we want to get them growing in their faith and impacting others right now. So the question is, how do we get them on the path of serving Jesus Christ?

THE MILLION-DOLLAR QUESTION

When it comes to convincing new believers of the importance of not only attending church but also serving Christ with all of their hearts, I have found the million-dollar question to be very useful. ✠

Once someone indicates faith in Jesus and I am convinced that the person understood the gospel message, I pop this powerful question, "If I were to give you a million dollars right now, would you slap me and walk away?" The person's answer usually goes something like, "Of course not." When I probe a little deeper and ask why, the new believer tells me, "Because I am grateful for your tremendous gift!" Then I ask another question, "God has just given you something of infinitely more value than a million dollars. He has given you eternal life! Are you going to slap Him in the face and walk away, or are you going to serve Him?" Every time the person's answer is "serve Him." "Why?" I ask. "Because I am grateful for His tremendous gift to me" is the inevitable response. ✠

The power of the million-dollar question is that it enables the new believer to understand that the reason we serve Jesus Christ is not a "have to" but a "want to." We serve Jesus not to prove our salvation, keep our salvation, or earn our salvation, but because of our salvation! Wholehearted service to and love for God flows out of a thankful heart. John the apostle put it this way, "We love (him) because he first loved us (1 John 4:19)." ✠

INVOLVEMENT IN THE CHRISTIAN COMMUNITY

Once you have asked the million-dollar question, invite the person you have led to Christ to attend youth group or a small group meeting with you. There is a much stronger likelihood that the person will attend a solid church if he or she has somebody to attend with. ⊠

Do your best to get the new believer plugged in to the body as soon as possible. The longer you wait, the stronger the possibility that the person will never be implanted into a church. ⊠

WORST-CASE WITNESSING SCENARIO #3
YOU HAVE BEEN SHARING YOUR FAITH FOR A LONG TIME AND REALIZE ONE DAY THAT YOU STILL AREN'T ANY BETTER AT IT THAN WHEN YOU FIRST STARTED.

One of the saddest things I see when it comes to teens sharing their faith is when they do it consistently but don't improve. God calls us to excel, improve, grow, and change. If you aren't doing that, then you could be like the believers in Hebrews 5:11–12, "We have much to say about this, but it is hard to explain because you are slow to learn. In fact, though by this time you ought to be teachers, you need someone to teach you the elementary truths of God's word all over again. You need milk, not solid food!" ✠

The goal for a baby's nutrition is to move from milk to meat. The goal for a believer when it comes to evangelism is to move from amateur to pro. This section of the chapter will help you to do that. Take a look at the graph on the next page and see the three levels of evangelistic skill. ✠

The goal is to move from an amateur to a rookie to a pro when it comes to sharing your faith. You can see from the graph the characteristics of each level. ✠

AMATEURS

The amateur is motivated but not trained. Amateurs love Jesus and want others to know Him, but sometimes they do more harm than good. Because they don't know what to say to effectively communicate the gospel, they either end up getting mad or turning quiet when confronted. Amateurs tend to talk in circles and not make a whole lot of sense when it comes to sharing the gospel. The key word to describe an amateur when witnessing is "ramble." Often these are new believers with an obvious excitement and love for Jesus. Although they may not know the right things to say, their enthusiasm can be contagious, and the obvious changes in their lives can be a reason for the friends who know them best to want what they have found. ✠

HOW TO IMPROVE YOUR SKILL

CLASSIFICATION		DESCRIPTION
LEVEL 1	AMATEUR	• Doesn't really know how to bring it up with strangers, friends, or family members. • Doesn't know how to explain the gospel to them either. • Sometimes does more harm than good.
LEVEL 2	ROOKIE	• Has mastered a specific technique / method of sharing the faith. • Knows it and shares it (sometimes "robotically").
LEVEL 3	PRO	• Can turn any conversation anytime toward the gospel. • Knows how to use questions skillfully to bring up spiritual matters. • Knows when to back off. • Doesn't dominate through dialogue but communicates through questions.

ROOKIES

Rookies are motivated and trained to share their faith. They have learned a pre-set method for sharing their faith like the 2.6.2 and know how to bring it up, spell it out, and wrap it up. If you have memorized and practiced the 2.6.2, then you are at the rookie level of sharing your faith. The challenge with this level is that everything is kind of pre-set and there is not a whole lot of room for creativity. Sometimes rookies tend to be robots in the way they witness. The key word in describing a rookie when witnessing is "talk." ▓

AT SHARING YOUR FAITH

KEYWORD	ACTION STEPS
RAMBLE	• Learn the 2.6.2 Technique (or other method). • Practice the 2.6.2 Technique. • Pick 2 opening questions that fit your personality and the situation. • Role-play.
TALK	• Personalize the 2.6.2 to your own style (add your own touch). • Share your story (before/during/after). • Look for opportunity in everyday conversation to "bring it up."
LISTEN	• Learn other techniques and methods of sharing your faith. • Discover how to mix and match. • Train others how to witness!

PROS

At the "professional" level you have mastered a method, personalized it, and practiced it to the point where you are not dependent on it. You always have your witnessing radar on and know how to use questions to turn a conversation toward the funnel and down the spout. You know when to charge ahead and when to back off. This is what I like to call the "Jesus level" of evangelism. Check out John 4 and see how Jesus turned a conversation about a cup of water into a witnessing experience in less than thirty seconds! The key word in describing a pro when witnessing is "listen."

MOVING FROM AMATEUR TO ROOKIE

If you want to move from an amateur to a rookie evangelist, then memorize and master the 2.6.2. Know it forward and backward. Practice it with your Christian friends, youth leader, campus ministry, and youth group. Personalize it and make it your own. Tie in your own story and your own illustrations. 🎴

TURNING PRO

If you want to turn into a pro evangelist, it takes these key factors:

SPIRITUAL MATURITY

The more you grow in your relationship with God, the better you can become at pro evangelism. You become sensitive to the Spirit of God and His leading in your heart. He will give you the wisdom you need to know when to back off and when to proceed. He will help you know which questions to ask. As you grow closer to God He will trigger your witnessing radar again and again and give you the wisdom you need to get the conversation into the funnel and down the spout. 🎴

TRIAL AND ERROR AND TIME

To be honest, becoming a pro evangelist is not an overnight thing. It takes a lot of effort. It comes with a whole lot of failure. 🎴

I have been actively sharing my faith since I was eleven years old, and I am still learning how to improve and what not to do. It is an ongoing process that never ends. Trial and effort and time are key ingredients as you "fail forward" to becoming a skilled and effective witness for Jesus Christ. ▧

ROLE-PLAYING

Role-playing is a key practice that can be developed to help turn you into a pro evangelist. In youth group or with strong Christian friends, plunge yourself into mock conversations where you seek to turn conversations toward the gospel. Take a subject like sports or astronomy or movies or music or Websites, and practice naturally making the transition toward spiritual subjects by asking questions. ▧

LISTENING

This is a key, key element in becoming a skilled pro evangelist. If you want to become effective at reaching others for Christ on the pro level, you must learn to listen. The rule of thumb is this: Once a person feels listened to and understood, then there is a strong possibility that the person will hear you out and try to understand your message. ▧

We must listen to people's words and what they are saying. But we must also try to listen to their hearts. We must seek to put ourselves in their shoes and empathize with them. The degree that we learn to listen is the degree that we will turn pro. ▧

4

WORST-CASE WITNESSING SCENARIO #4 YOU ARE WITNESSING TO A TEENAGER WHO DOESN'T TRUST IN JESUS CHRIST BECAUSE HE OR SHE IS CONFUSED BY THE TERMS THAT YOU ARE USING.

You have tried and tried to explain the gospel, but the person just doesn't get it. What do you do? Try to evaluate the terms you are using to share the gospel message and see if they are as clear as they can be. Maybe some of the terms you are using are confusing them. Let's take a look at some of the terms that we sometimes use when we communicate the gospel.

"ASK JESUS INTO YOUR HEART"

This expression is used in churches all across the globe to communicate how a person can become a Christian. This may be a term you remember hearing from your Sunday school teacher when you were little. Maybe it's the expression that God used to spark conversion in your spirit. But for many it strikes confusion, not conversion. Chalk me up as one of them.

I remember as a little kid in Sunday school at Bethany Baptist Church in downtown Denver hearing teacher after teacher calling me to "ask Jesus into my heart." But that term confused me. I thought (to my neurotic self), *What if I get a heart transplant or cough real hard? Will Jesus be gone for good? Will I still go to heaven?* I didn't understand the concept. Many children (and adults) don't. That term sparked confusion, not conversion, in my heart. ✖

Nowhere in the Bible does it say that we have to ask Jesus into our heart to be saved. The word that is used again and again to describe what we must do is "believe." This kind of belief is an active trust in Jesus and what He did on the cross. It doesn't mean that someone simply believes that Jesus existed and died on a cross, but that he or she is trusting in Him alone as the only hope for forgiveness. ✖

"TURN FROM ALL OF YOUR SINS"

I will never forget preaching at the Denver Rescue Mission as a young, nineteen-year-old "preacher boy." I knew that I literally had a captive audience. If these men and women wanted to eat and have a place to sleep that night, then they had to listen to my sermon. I also knew that they were used to hearing typical downtown "turn or burn" sermons. If they hadn't heard them at the rescue mission, they had heard them in the streets of Denver where curbside preachers wield their pointy fingers and push their pointed sermons. So I decided to try something different. ✖

As I stood behind the pulpit and looked at this room filled with the dysfunctional and drunk, I noticed that the rescue mission staff was sitting off to my left in some chairs along the wall. They, too, were used to hearing sermons. But they weren't prepared for what I was going to say. ❖

"How many of you in this room have ever heard a preacher tell you that if you want to go to heaven you have to give up your drinking, your smoking, your cussing, your chewing, your drugs, and your sexual immorality?" I started. They all kind of looked up with a groggy look of acknowledgment. Many raised their hands in affirmation and grunted out "I have." I went on, "Well, I want to tell you something a little different tonight." I will never forget that moment. Everybody looked up in confusion at once, including the rescue mission staff. ❖

"Here's what I want to tell you," I continued. "If you want to go to heaven, keep your alcohol, cigarettes, tobacco chew, drugs, and sexual sins." Talk about a cup of coffee to sober up everybody in the audience. Their eyes were wide open. Their jaws were dropped. By now the rescue mission staff was standing (ready to remove me from the pulpit). One of the disheveled men in the audience yelled out a hearty "Amen!" to my proclamation. ❖

Now that I had their full attention, I went on, "You keep every single one of your sins and you come to the cross of Jesus Christ. You simply believe that He died for those sins. You simply place your trust in Him to forgive you for those sins. And not only will He forgive you, but

He will come to live inside of you and He will give you the power and desire to turn from those sins. But you cannot turn from your sins until you have the power to do so. And you cannot have the power to do so until you are forgiven. And you cannot be forgiven until you believe." �ﬁ

The rescue mission staff sat back down. Seven or so people were transformed that night by the power of the gospel message. Jesus began turning them from their sin, and He will never give up until He has succeeded! ✶

Too many times Christians present a gospel with conditions. In the process the grace of God is cheapened by a focus on what we do rather than on what Christ has done. ✶

Simple and real faith in Jesus Christ is the only requirement to salvation given in the whole Bible, nothing more, nothing less. Some think that this way of salvation is way too easy. But how easy is it to stake your eternity on someone you have never met? How easy is it to trust fully in someone you have never seen? It is so easy that a child can do it, and it is so difficult a religious person can choke on it. ✶

"MAKE JESUS THE LORD OF YOUR LIFE"

Here is another phrase that can confuse those we are talking to about the gospel. As we are sharing the gospel message we must be very careful not to make it sound like people have to do something to receive it other than trust in Jesus Christ. When we say "You must make Jesus the Lord of your life to be saved," we are basically saying that faith is not enough, but that people must commit to serve Christ as well. As soon as we say that, we risk saying the same thing as the other religions that say you must do something to achieve eternal life. ✂

When people put their faith in the Lord Jesus Christ, they are saved into a relationship where they are commanded to obey Him. From that moment on they belong to God. We don't "make Him Lord," because He already is Lord. If we choose to serve our Lord, we will be blessed. When we choose not to serve Him, we will be disciplined by our loving and holy heavenly Father. But serving Him is not a requirement for salvation. It is a result of it. ✂

"JUST SAY THIS PRAYER AND YOU WILL BE SAVED"

Saying a prayer for salvation never saved anyone. It is simply a way for us to express to God the faith that has taken place in our hearts. Believe me, there are many people out there who have said the sinner's prayer and will end up in hell because they never truly trusted in Jesus Christ. They were going through the motions. Jesus never led anybody through the "sinner's prayer." Why? Because saying a prayer never saved anyone! ✂

Don't get me wrong. It's absolutely fine and good to get someone to pray with you. Just make sure they know that saying a prayer doesn't save them . . . their faith and trust in Jesus does. ✂

WORST-CASE
WITNESSING SCENARIO #5
YOU WANT TO WITNESS TO YOUR
FRIEND, BUT YOU CHICKEN OUT
AT THE LAST MINUTE.

We have all been there. I know that I have. You get yourself all psyched up to share the gospel with that friend, and the moment of truth arrives and you get scared and abort the mission. ✴

What do you do in this scenario? I think that this is when we need a huge reminder of our power source. You may know the 2.6.2 backward and forward. You may have role-played and practiced all the witnessing scenarios a person could possibly imagine. You may have mastered the truths in this book, but if you forget your power source, you are in trouble. ✴

Jesus' last words on earth were these, "But you will receive power when the Holy Spirit comes on you; and you will be my witnesses in Jerusalem, and in all Judea and Samaria, and to the ends of the earth" (Acts 1:8). That word *power* means "explosive power." It is a power that will blow us and others away! It will blast us past our fears and blast others into the kingdom of God. And all of that power flows from the Holy Spirit Himself. ✴

The Holy Spirit is the third person of the Trinity. He came to live inside of you the moment you put your faith and trust in Jesus Christ (Ephesians 1:13–14), and He will not leave you until you are safely in heaven with God. ❇

His mission is to give you power to live a life that pleases God and give you power to reach your world for Jesus Christ. He gives us the courage we need to live the life and spread the message. ❇

So how do you tap into the power of the Holy Spirit? Two things:

#1 PRAY

Ask God to take control of you through His Holy Spirit. As soon as you do, the Spirit of God takes the steering wheel of your heart, soul, and mind. You may not feel a thing, but just remember that it is not a matter of feeling. It is a matter of faith. ❇

If you have sinned, confess that sin to God so that the Spirit of God can control you. Unconfessed sin is like a rag stuffed in a water pipe. The water can't get out if you don't remove the rag. In the same way, if you have sin in your life that has not been dealt with, the Spirit of God can't flow through you with His mighty power. ❇

#2 TRUST

Trust in God's Spirit to give you all of the courage, strength, and wisdom you need to share your faith with your friends (or with strangers, for that matter). As you trust in Him He will guide you and encourage you and help you. Here's what Jesus told His disciples about the power of the Spirit working through us as we trust in Him: "At that time you will be given what to say, for it will not be you speaking, but the Spirit of your Father speaking through you" (Matthew 10:19–20). ✻

Every single day put your faith and trust in God's Spirit. Make a daily declaration of dependence on the Holy Spirit. As you do, you will be ready to face any worst-case witnessing scenario. ✻

STUDENT SURVIVAL TIPS

1. Memorize the argument buster, the million-dollar question, and the 4-1 defensive formation word for word.

2. Ask your youth leader whether he or she thinks that you are an amateur, a rookie, or a pro when it comes to sharing your faith.

3. Ask yourself how clear you are in your terms when it comes to sharing your faith. Do you use terms like "Say this prayer" or "Ask Jesus into your heart" or "Turn from all your sin"?

Worst-Case Scenario

You have shared the gospel with a friend who is an atheist. You have shared the 2.6.2 and used the 4-1 defensive formation. She still doesn't believe. As a matter of fact, her arguments are better than yours. She even knows more about the Bible than you do. It seems like for every argument you have, she has one that is better. You have showed the love of Christ but don't know how to get her to believe. What do you do?

The Tribal Challenge

Break up into groups of two and practice sharing the gospel in some more difficult situations. Try role-playing four different situations: talking to a Mormon friend, talking to an atheist teacher, talking to a Wiccan relative, and talking to a Muslim stranger. For a list of their beliefs, check out www.dare2share.org.

Soul Survivor

8

"Yes, I am coming soon."
Jesus (Revelation 22:20)

✳ Will your friends be soul survivors?
This may be your last chance to reach
them to save them from the judgment of

EARTH THAT IS JUST AROUND THE CORNER. JESUS IS COMING SOON, MAYBE SOONER THAN YOU THINK. WHEN HE RETURNS IT WILL BE TOO LATE FOR YOU TO REACH YOUR FRIENDS WITH THE GOSPEL OF JESUS CHRIST. AM I TRYING TO SCARE YOU? YOU BET I AM. �

There are some things about the coming of Jesus that we should be afraid *of* and there are some things that we should be afraid *for.* We should only be afraid of the return of Jesus Christ if we have not been serving Him as believers. When our eyes meet His, will we see the look of a proud father or a disappointed dad? ✻

We should be afraid for our friends who don't know Jesus Christ as their Savior. What they will go through if we don't reach them in time is the very judgment of the almighty God. That should scare us for them. ✻

But it's not just the coming of Jesus that should motivate us to reach our friends before it's too late. It's also the coming of graduation. ✻

You have a tiny window of opportunity to reach your friends while you are in school. After the tassel is moved on your cap and you receive that diploma, it is good-bye high school . . . and the vast majority of your high school friends. This is the best time to reach them— right now, not tomorrow, not a month from now, but right now. ✻

Satan wants you to wait. He whispers, "Wait a little longer. Let them see Jesus in your life and bring it up to you. I mean, come on, do you really think that they are ready to hear the gospel, anyway? Give them a little more time." ✻

But the days turn into months and the months into years and the years into regret. That's why I love the words of Charles Spurgeon. He lived more than a hundred years ago in England, but he was a radical. He loved teenagers. As a matter of fact, he was sixteen years old when he pastored his first church. By the age of nineteen he was pastoring the largest church in England! ✂

Mr. Spurgeon had a low tolerance for waiting around. He told a group of young men who were studying to be in the ministry,

Brethren, do something; do something; do something. While committees waste their time over resolutions, do something. While Societies and Unions are making constitutions, let us win souls. Too often we discuss, and discuss, and discuss, and Satan laughs in his sleeve. It is time we had done planning and sought something to plan. I pray you, be men of action all of you. Get to work and quit yourselves like men.[1]

Now is the time to go for it. Do something. Quit talking about it and start doing something about it. The souls of your friends hang in the balance. ✂

SOUL SURVIVAL
TRAINING FOR YOU

If you are going to make it in these confusing end times, you need some soul survival training for yourself. You need to make sure that you have a consistent personal time to mend your soul and build your internal strength. Without it you will crumble amidst the coming battles that you will face in this life.

There are two disciplines that you need to stay strong:

1 COMMUNE WITH YOUR GOD.

What does it mean to commune with your God? I challenge you to take some time and start flipping through the Psalms. Most of these "songs" were written by David as he communed with God. Some of them were written by him while he was on the run from his enemy, hiding in caves in the wilderness. Some of them were written by him when he was the king of Israel at his palace in Jerusalem. In other words, he wrote them in good times and bad. In good times he praised God for His blessings. In bad times he begged God for His help. The point is that in good times and bad David was in communion with the God he loved so much. Are you?

I am not talking about having "devotions" or a "quiet time." I am talking about being a devotion and living a quiet time. Every moment of every day should be an expression of praise to God Himself. Just like David we should be living and breathing our relationship with God. Our thoughts should stray to Him in the middle of the day. We should be dreaming about Him at night. Knowing Him should be our deepest passion and our highest goal.

The driving fire behind every great man and woman of God throughout history has been to know Jesus

Christ. Listen to the words of Paul, "What is more, I consider everything a loss compared to the surpassing greatness of knowing Christ Jesus my Lord, for whose sake I have lost all things. I consider them rubbish, that I may gain Christ" (Philippians 3:8). Do you sense what Paul is saying? Everything else is trash compared to knowing Christ. ❈

Being the best player on your team . . . trash. Getting a scholarship to college . . . trash. Your relationships . . . trash. Your friends, hobbies, car, clothes . . . trash, trash, and more trash. Compared to the privilege of knowing Christ intimately, everything else is trash. It's not that these other things don't matter. They do matter. It's just that *compared* to the pursuit of intimacy with Jesus they are all a big pile of garbage. ❈

This probably means that you have a daily time set aside that you just talk to God through prayer and that He talks to you through His Word. It probably means that you keep a journal of your walk with God. Maybe it means that you, like David, learn to write poetry to Him and prayers to Him in an expression of your desire for Him. But it means much, much more. It means a life that revolves around Him and pleasing Him. It means that every relationship, every habit, every homework assignment—everything—has one primary purpose, and that is to make God happy. ❈

2 COMMIT TO YOUR COMMUNITY.

Imagine a soldier without an army, a player without a team, an ember without a fireplace, and you can begin to imagine a Christian without a community. I am talking about being a part of the church, not going to church. There is a world of difference. Many if not most Christian teenagers go to church and never experience the church. ❈

You see, the church of the Bible was a community of believers who loved each other and served each other while learning, worshiping, praying, growing, and, yes, witnessing. The church of the Bible is not about a building but about a body . . . a body of believers who were passionately in love with each other, ruthlessly honest with each other, and fully committed to each other. ❈

Have you ever read the book of Acts and then gone to church? Talk about a letdown! The typical church today tends to be about programs and preaching and Sunday morning services. The early New Testament church was about fellowship and worship and outreach as well as preaching. Today many churches focus on building bigger buildings. Then the church focused on building better community. ❈

If you are going to be a soul survivor in these end times, it is going to take plugging into a community of believers at school and at church who will be able to encourage, confront, and build you. It is going to take a group of believing friends who know you inside out and can help you, and whom you can help. It is going to take being plugged into an intimate community of on-fire believers. If you want to be a soul survivor, it is going to take getting connected to your team. ✠

THE GREAT GRADUATION EVACUATION

Did you know that the vast majority of teenagers who are currently attending a church somewhere will evacuate the church completely after they graduate from high school? These pretenders never "owned" their own faith. Instead they have been borrowing it from Mom and Dad until they are no longer under their jurisdiction. For most Christian teenagers, graduation means a new phase of life in the workforce, party zone, or college dorm . . . minus their Christianity. ✠

Don't be a statistic! Commune with your God and commit to your community. Choose to be a soul survivor. ✠

JOIN THE E-TEAM REVOLUTION

The e-team revolution is a national movement of youth-group-based evangelism teams who are willing to do what it takes to reach their campuses and communities for Jesus Christ on a grass roots level. This nondenominational, multicultural movement is driven by this fundamental belief: The hope for America's spiritual future is rooted in the gospel being delivered by the youth of our churches. This means you! ✠

E-team stands for evangelism team. We have drama teams and worship teams in youth group; why not an evangelism team? �

This movement is based on small groups of revolutionary teenagers who are passionate about evangelism leading the way for the fulfillment of the Great Commission in their sphere of influence. The e-team revolution is directed by youth leaders who provide direction, guidance, support, and encouragement as student evangelists just like you seek to expand the kingdom of God. ✖

An e-team is a group of students operating within the typical youth ministry who are committed to energizing students in their youth group to evangelize their world (friends and students on campus). Using an invitational outreach strategy called Prayer-Dare-Share and other creative strategies, the e-teams lead the way for outreach and discipleship on a youth group level. ✖

YOUTH-GROUP-BASED

Unlike many other outreach strategies, the plan that drives the e-team centers around the main youth group meeting held by that particular church. That youth group meeting becomes the hub of the outreach efforts by the e-team and the entire youth group. Although these same principles can be applied to campus ministry outreach efforts, the youth group meeting is often overlooked as a key tool in reaching the unchurched with the gospel of Jesus Christ. ✖

INVITATIONAL EVANGELISM

Did you know that studies have shown that the majority of teenagers say they would go to church or youth group if invited by a friend? This means that if you and your e-team begin inviting lost friends out to youth group and you challenge and equip the other teens in your group to invite their lost friends out, they will come out! This is where they can see the gospel in action and hear the gospel message.

The e-team can be the trigger for the evangelism explosion and spiritual revival in the typical youth group, church, and community. Their primary goal is not merely addition but spiritual multiplication. Replicating an "Acts-like" culture of spiritual transformation is what drives the e-team. It's about much more than just witnessing. It's about awakening.

The e-team strategy centers around a pledge and a plan. The pledge is for the youth leader to commit to doing a high quality youth group meeting every week and to present the gospel at the end of every talk. This is essential so the students can know that anytime they bring unchurched friends into the context of the youth group meeting, they will hear a clear gospel presentation.

"The first thing Andrew did was to find his brother Simon and tell him, 'We have found the Messiah' (that is, the Christ). Then he brought Simon to Jesus" (John 1:41–42). Operation Andrew is what the Billy Graham Evangelistic Association calls it. Invitational evangelism is what others call it. The Prayer-Dare-Share Strategy is what Dare 2 Share Ministries calls it. But no matter what it is titled, the principle is the same: Friends inviting friends to a place where they can meet Jesus is the simple plan. �֎

Andrew invited his brother to a place where he could meet Jesus. It was "the first thing Andrew did" after meeting Jesus himself. Automatically Andrew had the urge to evangelize. Why? Good news is contagious! ✖

THE PRAYER-DARE-SHARE STRATEGY

This simple strategy is called Prayer-Dare-Share. It is built around your e-team's setting the pace for invitational evangelism among all of your students. It all centers on the epicenter of your weekly youth ministry meeting. ✖

PRAYER:

Students begin praying for their lost friends. You and your youth group pray by name for your friends who don't know Jesus. The e-team sets the pace, but everybody is involved. ✖

DARE:

You and your friends invite (dare) your friends to come out to the youth group meeting (where they will hear a clear gospel presentation from the youth leader). These invitations are consistent, almost daily, until the lost student agrees to come out to youth group. This invitational evangelism is persistent and passionate. It involves training other teenagers in your youth ministry to become talking billboards for the youth group meeting. ❖

SHARE:

The inviting students share the gospel with the invited students afterward by asking simple and straightforward follow-up questions, "Did what my youth leader say make sense?" and "Based on what he/she said, do you know for sure that you are going to heaven when you die?" ❖

Across America almost every youth group that is surging numerically is doing some form of this invitational strategy. Churches that are surging numerically have this in common as well. High quality meetings combined with an invitational strategy combined with a gospel presentation leads to evangelistic effectiveness. The *prayers* prepare their hearts to hear the gospel. The *dares* convince them to come. And the *share* makes sure they have an understanding of the gospel message given during the meeting. ❖

This e-team is comprised of at least five key roles (we encourage at least ten participants in these key roles, if your group is large enough) who commit to meet weekly to keep one another accountable in the area of youth-group-based evangelism, to learn from God's Word how to become better leaders of the cause, and to meet at least monthly to creatively brainstorm how to become more effective as an e-team. Below is a graph of what the basic concept of the e-team looks like. ⌘

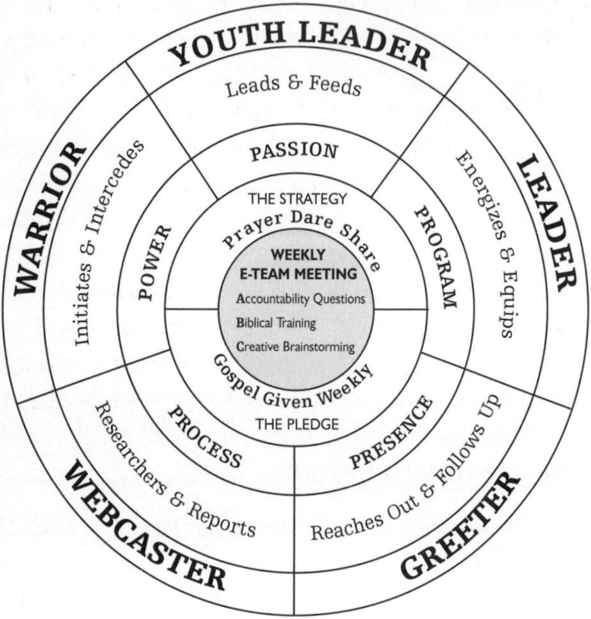

There is really a limitless number of students who can be involved in one of these roles. For instance, you could have from three to thirty students participating as prayer warriors. The same is true of the greeters. You could even have more than one Webcaster and leader. As a matter of fact, everyone in your youth group can be on the e-team if they are committed to the cause. Now that's a revolution! ⌘

THE ADULT YOUTH LEADER

The youth leader **leads and feeds.** He or she is responsible to lead the rest of the youth group to an evangelistic mind-set and feed the e-team through a weekly e-team meeting. This doesn't necessarily need to be the youth pastor. This position can be filled by a skilled adult sponsor who is passionate about evangelism. This youth leader provides the passion for the evangelistic movement in the youth group. Students have a tendency to get distracted and discouraged when it comes to evangelistic effectiveness. So it is these youth leaders who fan the embers back into flames. This youth leader must be making sure that the evangelism thrust is growing, and that more and more students are becoming involved and excited about evangelism. ✕

THE STUDENT LEADER

The leadership role is filled by at least one student who **energizes and equips** the rest of the students in the area of evangelism. There can be more than one leader. The leaders train the rest of the youth group in the strategy and methods of effective evangelism and spiritual reproduction. Leaders are responsible for the evangelism training program. Under the leadership of the youth leader, the student leaders motivate the rest of the group through giving public challenges, personal testimonies, and powerful training. They will be the ones giving the call from the front to evangelistic outreach and spiritual awakening. Maybe that means a weekly time of testimony and motivation in front of the rest of the youth group. Maybe that means you let them teach a few lessons on evangelism every quarter. Whatever it looks like in your youth ministry culture, the leadership team is the group of students who are the primary equipping evangelists in your youth ministry: They motivate the rest of the youth group by taking the lead. 🏵

THE GREETERS

"Obnoxiously friendly" are the words you want to remember when it comes to these teens! Their job is to **reach out and follow up.** They create an environment that is so upbeat, so friendly, and so genuine that lost students can't help but show up and come back (hopefully as saved students). This team makes visiting and returning teens feel comfortable from the moment they come through the doors. They meet them and greet them and they do much, much more. They may introduce them to other students, participate with them in the youth group games, sit next to them during the meeting, and overall make them feel comfortable. These greeters need to be teens who like everyone, and not ones who will hang around only with kids who wear the right clothes and present a "cool" image. If they aren't very friendly toward "geeky" new kids, those new kids will sense it, and others in the youth group might not include the uncool kids either. 🏵

These are the same students who follow up the meeting by kicking off the discipleship process. The key is getting the new believers to get involved with the youth group over the long haul. In other words, we want kids to get saved and then get plugged in to the community of believers. This is where Three Way Discipleship comes into play. This is the strategy that centers the key evangelistic and discipleship efforts of a youth group around invitations. �

The principle behind Three Way Discipleship is simple: The same relationship that convinced a student to visit the youth group in the first place is the best relationship to maximize discipleship efforts and get that student plugged in to the body of Christ over the long haul. It involves the greeter initiating the discipleship process with a newcomer through the student who invited the new student to the youth group in the first place. ✻

THE WEBCASTERS

The Webcasters **research and report.** These students are responsible to gather evangelistic, apologetic, and campus outreach resources for the entire youth group. They are to keep in contact with other students and share stories, stats, encouragement, and resources via e-mail. These students can connect the entire youth group with a Web-based approach to evangelism. ✻

One of the great things about the Webcaster is that he or she doesn't have to be the most social of people. This leaves ample room for a teen or small group of "Webheads" to make a difference evangelistically in the youth group. ✻

There is even a place on the Dare 2 Share Website (www.dare2share.org) for Webcasters to report weekly and let us know what is going on evangelistically in their youth groups and share ideas with other e-teams across America. The results? Every participating youth group is sharing ideas for the common cause of the advancement of the gospel of Jesus Christ through an army of teenagers. �֍

When Webcasters report to Dare 2 Share Ministries (www.dare2share.org), they tell which outreach ideas are working the best. These ideas in turn are shared with youth groups across America, and the revolution begins. Youth groups from across America are helping each other reach more students for Jesus. Methodist, Episcopal, Baptist, Lutheran, Presbyterian, Pentecostal, and nondenominational unite together via the Webcasters and launch the revolution by sharing information on the Dare 2 Share Website and Dare 2 Share e-mail blasts. ✖

THE WARRIORS

These students are the heart and soul of the e-team. There should be at least three prayer warriors that launch this movement in your youth group. They **initiate** a prayer movement and **intercede** for the lost friends of specific students by name. They not only are the intercessors, but they are the champions of intercession. They pray for lost students by name, and they challenge each student in the group to pray for lost students by name. These prayer warriors may lead concerts of prayer, fasts, or prayer chains for the lost. Their primary purpose is to pray specifically for lost students on a daily basis and to call on each teen in the participating youth group to pray for a list of students who they know don't know Christ. ✂

The whole youth group can be an e-team!

I hope you are getting this. The e-team is not an exclusive team for the best few students. It works best when it is an entire youth group effort. Your whole youth group can be a part of this e-team revolution! You can have an army of prayer warriors, Webcasters, greeters, and leaders! Maybe you elect a few of them in each role to meet weekly to brainstorm and pray, but the whole youth ministry can be involved! ✂

When I was a teenager I was part of an "e-team" of sorts. There were more than one hundred of us! We all were greeters and prayer warriors and leaders (no Webcasters back then, no Internet back then). At one point we had about eight hundred students in our youth ministry. When someone came in and trusted Christ, we would get the person to join the "e-team" as soon as possible. Some never did. Some did right away. It was awesome! ✂

So don't think that the e-team is just for the few and the chosen. It is for anyone and everyone who wants to reach friends for Jesus Christ! It is for anyone who wants to pay the price and reach the goal. For more information on how to launch the e-team revolution in your youth ministry, check out www.dare2share.org. ✂

RAPTURED WITH A BANG

I am convinced that the future of the church depends on you . . . that's right, you. Did you know that every major awakening in America had teenagers on the leading edge of that movement?

The typical church in America sees only two people come to Christ per year. That's it. At this pace we will never reach this country, let alone this world, with the gospel of Jesus Christ. It's time for a student-led awakening of biblical proportions in our churches.

It is time for a new breed of Christian who has a heart that beats hard after God, a mind that is drenched in His Word, a knee that is bent in prayerful dependence on His Spirit, a life that is a living example of Jesus, and a mouth that just won't shut up. We need a generation of teenagers to set the pace for our churches. We need a revolution of biblical proportions to unleash the contagious message of Jesus Christ all over this world.

Why? Because Jesus is coming back soon to rapture His church. My prayer is that when that trumpet blast sounds your friends are all reached with the message of the gospel and you have led the way for revival in your church. My prayer is that an army of teen revolutionaries has changed the face of the body of Christ. My prayer is that every person in every nation has heard the gospel message because of an army of Spirit-filled, gospel-proclaiming, unstoppable teenagers. My prayer is that because of you the church is raptured with a bang and not a whimper.

NOTE
1. C. H. Spurgeon, *Lectures to My Students* (Lynchburg, Va.: Old-Time Gospel Hour, 1875), 36.

SINCE 1894, Moody Publishers has been dedicated to equip and motivate people to advance the cause of Christ by publishing evangelical Christian literature and other media for all ages, around the world. Because we are a ministry of the Moody Bible Institute of Chicago, a portion of the proceeds from the sale of this book go to train the next generation of Christian leaders.

If we may serve you in any way in your spiritual journey toward understanding Christ and the Christian life, please contact us at www.moodypublishers.com.

"All Scripture is God-breathed and is useful
for teaching, rebuking, correcting and training in
righteousness, so that the man of God may be
thoroughly equipped for every good work."
—*2 TIMOTHY 3:16, 17*

MOODY
PUBLISHERS

THE NAME YOU CAN TRUST